Diversity Conversations

Finding Common Ground

2nd Edition

Eric M. Ellis, M.A.

www.integritydev.com

Diversity Conversations

Table of Contents

Foreword

I like what Diversity Conversations is setting out to do, and think its perspectives are fresh and authentic. I believe the book will be of substantial help to a large number of people who are open to examining their own attitudes toward diversity and who are committed to the belief they can lead more productive and satisfying lives by appreciating the differences in people and their opinions.

I particularly appreciated the insights that grow from examining the "conversations" we have on diversity with ourselves, with those who are like us, and with those who are not. The final chapter, which describes the process of becoming a diversity critical thinker is mind-opening and practical.

This is an honest book loaded with learnings and insights expressed in real-world terms. It will be a rare reader who leaves this book without being more aware of his or her own beliefs and better able to appreciate those of others and, as a result, being able to live a more satisfying life.

John E. Pepper,
Retired Chairman & CEO,
The Procter & Gamble Company and
Retired Chairman, The Walt Disney Company

Dedication and Acknowledgments

I dedicate this book first and foremost to my wife and best friend, Judy. Her love has given me the confidence to utilize every gift and talent I have to make a difference in the lives of others. Judy left her promising career at Procter & Gamble to invest her talents in raising our children. I love and respect her as a treasure from God. I also devote this book to our four children: Jillian, Eric II, Evan and Ethan. The courage and integrity my children have displayed, gives me confidence that they have what it takes to make a difference in this world for years to come. My family has been a mirror through which I regularly learn about my strengths and shortcomings.

My father, the late Dr. Duke E. Ellis (1933-1982) was a pioneer in diversity research and my first teacher. My mother, the late Rev. Rebecca Ford Ellis (1935-2010) was an evangelist and pioneer for other female preachers. This book is dedicated to carrying on their legacies.

I honor all my mentors, friends, consultants, and staff who have helped me on this journey towards life-long learning. I especially want to thank Floyd and Jackie Dickens, who were the first couple to believe in me beyond my parents and were the founders of 21st Century Management Services, Inc., the company that gave me my start in business. I appreciate Dr. Jeanette Taylor for hiring and mentoring me after graduate school. I am so thankful to Ray

Brokamp, the former Superintendent of Cincinnati Public Schools. A dear friend and mentor who was instrumental in hiring me as the Managing Director for INROADS. His genuine kindness led me to design and lead the diversity experience for the Leadership Cincinnati Program for recognized Executives, for almost two decades. You couldn't find two finer people in the world than Ray and his late wife, Pauline Brokamp (one of God's angels). My final dedication is to you. I hope this book motivates, encourages, and empowers you to find common ground as you build your experiences with diversity.

Introduction

As the great-great-grandson of a white Irishman, the great-grandson of a Native American, and the grandson of an African-American sharecropper from Cayuga, Illinois, I am also the child of one of the pioneers in the field of Diversity and an evangelical female preacher. Like you, my family's history has shaped my values, morals, and established the foundation of who I am today-- a diversity professional, husband, father, and friend.

The adversarial and at times hostile conversations about diversity have been some of the greatest struggles in our country since beginning work in this arena during the early 1980s. Over the past decade, admittedly, I have been writing this book in my head. Yet, the toxic political environment seemed to create enough frustration that I became totally committed to completing this book. It feels as though we are experiencing a whole new level of anger, misunderstanding, and name-calling from radical as well as mainstream America.

Following President Obama's election, people would jokingly ask me what I was going to do, since there would be less need for the Diversity Consulting Services we've provided for major organizations for more than two decades. Well, I must report that, unfortunately, I still have to work even harder. And as far as a post-racial society in America, we are nowhere close to the end of unpleasant conversations about diversity; conversations about diversity will remain as long as people are born.

Another impetus that fueled my engine to publish this book was my great concern for America. Far too often American citizens are being manipulated like pawns on a chessboard. I am often disappointed and saddened as people, many close friends, are deceived by Professional Diversity Polarizers (PDPs). So, my response is this resource to arm people with practical information so they can better understand diversity in general. Specifically, this book provides tools to recognize and reduce the conflict people experience surrounding discussions about diversity. This toolbox enables you, the reader, to take advantage of the best input from people who hold various points of view.

I have poured my soul and years of experience onto each page. A specific diversity story precedes each chapter, in order to remind the reader to continuously relate our content to practical everyday experiences. The chapters are set up to pose several key questions and then provide some perspective in response to those questions. The book is filled with relevant examples from discussions with literally thousands of Americans I have trained on diversity over the past three decades. Each chapter offers practical tips to increase effectiveness in conducting productive and critical diversity conversations with your friends, family, co-workers, and with your foes and people who do not view the world like you. My objective is that this book will provide you with a meaningful perspective on how to think critically about diversity in order to establish more productive discussions when human differences are involved. This book also prepares you to become more aware of the challenges we face as a nation as a result of political and cultural manipulation. It is critically important we raise our awareness so we can actively take part in this national and international conversation. As you become more aware of the multiple diversity conversations you have, you can avoid being led into dysfunctional and destructive cultural conflicts.

The three major Diversity Conversations we will explore:

- Diversity Conversations with Ourselves (Chapter 2)

- Conversations that people have with themselves (and their thoughts) about diverse people, issues, and points of view.

- Diversity Conversations with Like Others (Chapter 3)

- Conversations people have with those who may view diverse people, issues, or perspectives in ways similar to themselves.

- Diversity Conversations with Diverse Others (Chapter 4)

- Conversations people have with those who see people, issues, and points of view in ways that differ from themselves.

Chapter 5 helps you recognize some of the challenges we face when discussing and working through diversity issues. In this chapter, you will learn more about the strategies that Professional Diversity Polarizers (PDPs) often employ to recruit and maintain their listeners as loyal followers of their positions irrespective of its truth and or validity. Like the political figure who may change his position on an issue, you must continuously be in search of the objective truth and firmly stand on your core values and principles, even if it means going against the grain. In other words, your number one loyalty should be to the truth according to your understanding. As your understanding changes, by gathering other people's viewpoints, your positions might change as well. From a national perspective and like a politician's oath to his/her constituents, our long-term security and viability are dependent upon our ability to embrace information and insights brought forth from people who oftentimes are different. The final chapters of the book, chapters 6-7, prepare you with valuable tools and skills to more critically think about issues related to human differences. Because the nature of diversity-related conversations is often times so emotionally charged, it is difficult for people to objectively determine where they should stand on important issues. We offer in chapter six, a Seven Step Diversity Critical Thinking R.E.S.P.E.C.T process to assist readers in finding common ground with those in which they have a different perspective. We must break these patterns, and this book is offered as one resource. If people had more awareness of the three diversity conversations presented here, they would be better prepared to add more value to our national discourse on these critical societal issues. I am not simply trying to recruit more people to my side. On the contrary, more people should want to be liberated from the mindless rhetoric formed by the systems that have raised us, educated us, trained us, and sometimes even sought to control us. This 2nd Edition of Diversity Conversations includes a PowerPoint presentation of many of the main points in this book. We are doing as much as we can to ensure that a broad audience of people benefit from many of the concepts presented in this book.

When people are free to think critically for themselves, they will not line up neatly with other people who simply look like them, speak their same language, or were raised with similar values and belief systems. Readers of this book will be able to objectively explore numerous points-of-view without fear of losing themselves. As a person of strong personal faith, I am compelled to declare my greatest loyalty and strongest allegiance to three simple, but profound words highlighted in our Declaration of Independence: We the People. I stand with you as we each work to reduce the destructive power of ignorance as it seeks to indiscriminately pit us one against another simply because we are different. Each of us as individuals, are in search of a common hope, for a better tomorrow; for ourselves and those who follow us. Thank you for reading this book and having the courage and vision to invest time and energy in developing your knowledge, skills, and conversations about diversity.

Diversity Story Chapter 1

"Without Saying One Word"

I entered Forest Park High School as a 5'6", 99 lb., freshman. I was so excited to be attending my neighborhood high school. Forest Park, Ohio was a community in cultural transition during the 70's and 80's. During this period, over 70% of the students were of a race different than my own. By the time I was a junior, I had developed some amazing friendships with diverse students at my school.

I decided to run for student council in my senior year. I had never run for any kind of student government position in the past, so this was a very different experience for me. I truly believed in the value of diversity, so I invited a friend of mine, Wade Harlan, who happened to be white, to run with me as my Vice President. Now my opponent was very confident in himself. On the day we were scheduled to give our campaign speeches at school, I was on a field trip with my class and we didn't return in time to give my speech. The election was the next day so I missed the opportunity to speak to my classmates and had to depend on our ground game. My VP and I spoke with as many students as we could personally, asking them for their votes.

I'll never forget my opponent saying to me on Election Day, how unfortunate it was that I didn't get to give my speech, because that would have made it a closer race. He offered his condolences and then returned to shaking hands and giving away bubble gum victory cigars throughout the school day. The election was being held at lunchtime and the winner would be announced at the end of the day. When the Principal came on the public address system to announce the results, I must admit, I was very nervous. I listened attentively as they announced that my Vice President and I had won the election. This victory made me the first African-American student to be elected President of a Senior Class in school history. So one might say, (tongue and cheek) that before there was a Barack Obama, there was Eric Ellis. Without one word, I was voted into the history books, not because of my race, but because my fellow students believed in my leadership ability.

Chapter

1

In the Beginning was Diversity

"Diversity conversations always end in a comma"

In the beginning, God created the heavens and the earth. On the sixth day, God created humankind. For some people, these words are viewed simply as a fable from a religious book, while for others, they represent an irrefutable truth, not open to debate. You do not have to talk to a person very long to identify areas you see dramatically differently. Yet, our divergent ideas, values, beliefs and actions are based upon the fact that each of us is born a unique individual, unlike any other person in the world.

Take a minute to think about a situation in your life where you thought you had a complete grasp of the facts. Think about a time when you were confident about a perspective you held, only to learn you were wrong. I remember growing up believing that my father was much more reasonable than my mother. It wasn't until I was in college that I began to recognize how he would present an issue so his perspective seemed more legitimate. As I matured, I was better equipped to see through his tactics, and recognize the validity of many of my mother's perspectives. It is important that people develop an ability to be independent, critical thinkers. This skill can help you avoid falling prey to the various agendas set by others.

Diversity tends to be a very emotional subject and strong emotions can make it difficult to recognize the value of opposing points of view. It is critical that people understand how diversity is defined and the challenges we face as we seek to identify solutions to the common problems we face.

Diversity can be defined in as many different ways as there are people in the world. A simple definition we present in our workshops is, "human differences that make each individual unique."

di·verse (d $\bar{\imath}$-vûrs ; d $\bar{\imath}$-, d $\bar{\imath}$ vûrs)adj.
1. Differing one from another.
2. Made up of distinct characteristics, qualities, or elements

Utilizing differences to create conflict between people is as old as civilization itself. Diversity practitioners seek to understand the natural clusters through which people are identified, understood, and judged. We are constantly trying to determine how people's lives are influenced by their group affiliations. We will debate until the end of time whether or not people's life experiences are, in part, a result of how others view them, or how they see themselves. Is the quality of their life impacted by their group affiliations, or a result of their personal, social, and cultural traits?

Diversity draws much of its strength from people aligning themselves with others who have common traits. These individuals coalesce to fight common battles. Gangs are formed, battles are fought and people give their lives in support of the values and interests of their groups.

This chapter will provide an overview of the concept of diversity, its definition, its characteristics, and its influence on our thinking and daily conversations in America and throughout the world.

As an educator and speaker on the subject of diversity for a quarter of a century, I have had the opportunity to train tens of thousands of people from a broad cross section of diverse backgrounds. It has been my honor to listen to people express their heartfelt struggles and opinions about how diversity has impacted their daily lives. There has been broad agreement among various participants over the years that the media has had a lot to do with our biased view of others. One participant recently stated he felt as though we are simply, "One good speaker away from creating the same climate which existed in Hitler's Germany". His statement may sound to many as an unfair comparison or even an exaggeration. I am not sure we can easily dismiss his statement. Clearly, we have to be aware of those people, systems and tools, that seek to unfairly influence our view of others. It also appears that our increased appetite for the sensational has energized those who enjoy tearing down their philosophical opponents. Unfortunately, the average person is unwilling to challenge those who espouse counterproductive, ethnocentric rhetoric.

One of my major concerns is that people who are skillful at proselytizing the masses through their harmful rhetoric are manipulating ordinary people. For example, media outlets, political pundits, and social or political activists, encourage people to trust them and not those who have a different worldview. There are several objective indicators from interdisciplinary researchers (Lau et. al, Cohen, Garramone et.al.) documenting the overwhelming success negative advertising has had on people's views of political candidates. It is painful to watch people being pitted against one another. Our communities pay the price as various cultural, social, and political interest groups work to support and strengthen their own agendas while attacking those with a different worldview.

It is clearer to me today than at any other time in my life that diversity impacts everyone. It took many years to recognize the inherent truth of this statement. The majority of my life did not prepare me to understand this truth because the people I lived around were generally like me. I grew up believing I could only be the victim of negative diversity encounters and not a biased perpetrator because of the color of my skin. It has been easier to identify ways in which I have been marginalized or left out as opposed to how I have excluded or discriminated against others. Today, one of the most successful strategies we use in our diversity workshops revolves around the use of empathy. When people are asked to identify an example of a time when they were excluded for being different, they are far more receptive to learning about the ways in which others, different from themselves, have been discriminated against. As people connect with the negative feelings they experienced, they have more empathy for others experiencing similar challenges.

Dr. Martin Luther King Jr. said that we are inextricably bound to one another. From a very early age, however, it is normal for people to have an abundance of narcissistic love. Freud described this love as a normal part of being human, but if taken to extremes, this egotistical behavior can make it difficult for people to develop meaningful relationships with others. In my experience, most people grow up with the mind-set of looking out for themselves. Many individuals have a survival mentality and are generally focused on answering the question, "What's in it for me?" When I was a child, if there were two pieces of my favorite German chocolate cake, I would take the bigger piece and leave the smaller one for one of my siblings. This is a part of our natural response system. As we recognize diversity's universal impact on each of us, we will become more invested in identifying solutions that are acceptable to a wide variety of people, regardless of our differences.

As we begin to recognize the important idea that diversity impacts everyone, we will move away from arguing with each other over differences. Effectively interacting with others includes working through a vast array of diverse belief systems that have been shaped by each individual's unique life experiences. None of us is simply one-dimensional. Each of us possess some dominant cultural characteristics (those personal traits that have power and privilege) and other traits, that are not embraced (and at times are excluded) by the larger society.   The overarching benefit of diversity is that it seeks to ensure that everyone has a fair opportunity to achieve their full potential. Simply stated, as people reach their full potential, each of us is rewarded and we benefit from the gifts each person gives to society.

Diversity Defined

My father led hundreds of sensitivity training workshops at corporations like Procter & Gamble, General Electric, Ford Motor Co. and General Motors. Dr. Duke Ellis has been credited by many as establishing the firm that coined the term diversity. Marilyn Loden and Judy Rosner have also contributed substantially to the field of diversity with their concepts of primary and secondary dimensions of diversity. Primary dimensions are defined as differences we are born with, like race, gender and age. Secondary dimensions are social dimensions like marital status, parental status, and educational background (Loden, 1990). Now I call on you to understand your primary and secondary dimensions. Take out a piece of paper and identify your primary dimensions on the left side of the sheet and your secondary dimensions on the right side of the paper. Which list is longer and why do you think that is the case? Loden and Rosner's research centered on two dimensions of diversity: personal and social. During my research and training, another dimension was identified: organizational. Now a 3-dimensional model called 'The Universal Diversity Impact Model', influences each aspect of the lives of all people.

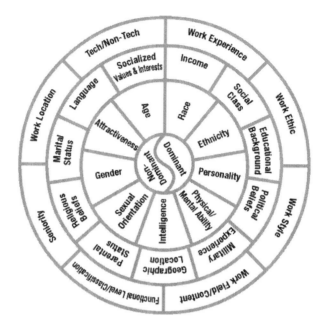

Figure 1.1

The Universal Diversity Impact Model

The Universal Diversity Impact Model highlights three levels of diversity. The characteristics included within the inner ring are described as the personal dimensions of Diversity (Loden, 1990). These traits are generally viewed as innate or immutable (traits we are born with like race, gender, etc.). The collection of traits in the middle ring is defined as social dimensions of diversity (Loden, 1990). They are socially based depending upon the affiliation people have with others in similar situations. These characteristics are viewed as fluent. In other words, they can change over the course of one's life. Examples may include a membership in a fraternity or sorority, police department or a parent-teacher organization. The outer ring is defined as organizational dimensions of diversity. These are typically distinctions that distinguish people within organizations. This includes your classification or job title, your level of expertise, and/or the experience you bring to the organization.

The Universal Diversity Impact Model is not a static model, but one that can change over time. Its purpose is simply to help us identify some of the ways individuals categorize themselves or others. The ultimate objective of the model is to discover how we view ourselves and others and how our similarities and differences impact our ability to live and work together effectively. The center of the wheel has two concepts that further aid in recognizing how these broad traits influence individuals, sub-groups, and our society in general.

Within any diverse population, there are dominant cultural traits and non-dominant cultural traits. Dominant cultural traits are those that have more power and privilege within a society. Non-dominant cultural traits are those that have less power and privilege within a society. If you study religion as a characteristic in the United States, you find that Christianity is the dominant culture trait. If your religious beliefs are different than Christians and you live in the United States, there are fewer privileges available to you. Generally, Americans do not attach the negative actions of other Christians to their faith. Unfortunately many Muslims have been negatively stereotyped as a result of the September 11, 2001 attacks.

Three Diversity Conversations

There are three Diversity Conversations that will be thoroughly explored throughout this resource. The first conversation is the one we have with ourselves; the second is the one we have with others like ourselves; and the third is the one we have with others different from us. Each conversation we have with others or ourselves is influenced by human differences. Ultimately, the conversation that seems to be the most divisive is the one that takes place between people who are unlike one another. In order to improve the level of respect during conversations with those who are different, you must improve the conversations people have with themselves and others who are similar philosophically, demographically, socially and politically.

The Value of a Broad Definition of Diversity

When I first started conducting diversity workshops, I felt my job was to be a Diversity *"Ghost Buster"*. The movie *Ghost Busters* was a very successful comedy in 1984 starring Dan Aykroyd and John Belushi. Their job was to go into homes with their special equipment to capture and rid the residences of ghosts. So when I started doing diversity workshops in the late 1980s, I felt like my job was to go into organizations and identify the racist, sexist, and homophobic attitudes, then bottle them up, and get them out of the organization. I was supposed to be the enlightened, bias-free trainer who saves the organization from the few prejudiced, mean-spirited, narrow-minded people.

In many ways, diversity training seminars from the 1980s and 1990s encouraged participants to play one of two roles. If you were white, you played the role of the villain, or perpetrator of discrimination, while minority participants played the victims of discrimination. Ultimately, success was reached when white participants confessed their "isms" and described their "aha" moment of understanding. Another major pathway to success was when minority participants expressed examples of being excluded and described the pain it caused.

In the early years of training, using this conflict-oriented approach to "solve" diversity issues, we may have used charts that defined diversity broadly, but people didn't believe we were having a genuine conversation until we were dealing with other topics outside of race and gender. There was great value gained from these very difficult conversations. When done well, these workshops achieved powerful results.

Over time, our workshops transitioned to honestly embracing a broader definition of diversity. Ultimately, there are significant benefits from honestly recognizing that all people have characteristics of the dominant culture (the power culture) and other traits that make them part of the non-dominant culture (less power and privilege). This was an epiphany for me personally, and forms my training and research today. From this evolution, there are four key benefits to defining diversity more broadly.

Diversity is Fundamentally Broad

Diversity is all the ways in which we are unique. People naturally gravitate to others who possess characteristics that are similar to their own. This yields a large number of sub-groups that often band together to accomplish similar objectives. Ultimately, diversity has to be focused on insuring that all people are meaningfully included in our society and the institutions that comprise our communities.

Diversity is Inclusive

In short, diversity includes more people. From my initial workshops, there was great value in creating empathy. We often use a video called *'The Tale of O'* produced by Rosa Beth Moss Kantor, a Harvard professor. Kantor studied women entering corporate America for the first time. She used an animation that depicted *X*'s as the dominant cultures and *O*'s as the non-dominant culture. Although her research was initially focused on the dynamics of women joining a predominantly male environment, the exercises that followed invited all participants to identify times when they themselves were very different than a majority group. As people had the opportunity to share their own experiences of being ostracized, minimized and left out, they were more receptive to listening to and understanding some of the challenges faced by people who were different from them in their own organizations.

Eliminates Barriers of a Narrow Definition

If diversity is defined within confining parameters, it becomes hard to garner and sustain support from the larger society, especially other groups who view themselves as excluded or even harmed by the existence of diversity initiatives. The advancement of the Civil Rights Movement paved the way for the Women's Rights Movement, and the Gay and Lesbian Rights Movement. In other words, there would be greater criticism and resistance to the value of the Civil Rights Movement, if it had not resulted in opening doors for other disenfranchised groups. Diversity has to work on solving the problems of all groups of people who are being excluded in order to survive. Therefore, a narrow definition makes it hard for some people to receive the message and become engaged in solving the problems of others.

A Broad Definition of Diversity Creates Equity

It is valuable for all participants to come to a workshop to learn something. Participants do not need to play just a victim or a perpetrator; but realize that these dynamics exist within all people. There is clearly a reality of the dominant culture across all societies. Generally speaking, the dominant culture in a society still has more power and privilege than the non-dominant culture. But each individual, irrespective of group affiliation, must recognize their own socialization, prejudices, and biases and how they influence their behavior towards others. A broad definition of diversity allows all people to connect with their experiences as both victims and perpetrators. This helps to create a sense of equity in diversity conversations. It also challenges everyone to own personal biases and become committed to change.

The Downsides of a Broad Definition of Diversity

Although my training highlights the positive aspects of having a wide definition of diversity, there are individuals who disagree with this approach due to the following reasons.

A broad definition of diversity can make the conversation seem unnecessary or overwhelming. I have heard people say in different workshops, "If everybody is different, why do we need to have this conversation?" It's important to be aware that a broad definition of diversity enables some people to make light of the entire area of focus. People do not want to have to deal with the complexity of diversity. They are seeking a quick, fast and simple solution to the problem.

Fairness & Equity can seem unattainable

A broad definition of diversity can make goals of fairness and equity seem unattainable. My overall experience has been that people generally feel a workshop delivers greater value when the issues being discussed are ones that impact them directly, not just a laundry list of politically correct issues.

People can avoid uncomfortable diversity topics

Oftentimes, people are not comfortable addressing issues of discrimination and inequity. No one likes to feel as though they have received benefits they did not earn or be blamed for inequalities of the past. Other people simply don't want people who are different to have to hear they are being treated unfairly. Therefore, a broad definition of diversity allows people to change the subject. People are often very uncomfortable discussing biases they have toward others who are different. When the conversation becomes broad, they can avoid topics that make them the most uncomfortable. This often leads to stagnation in their personal growth.

The Cost of Counterproductive Diversity Conversations

If someone had to record and justify the costs related to fighting over our differences, these behaviors would decrease significantly. The personal and societal costs are disconcerting because they place us at great risk as a civilization. When I was growing up, I must admit I was not a big fan of reading. However, when I was in the ninth grade, there was one book we read, *Animal Farm* that I'll never forget. At the time, it seemed so innocent and ordinary. There were animals from different backgrounds and different places, who ended up on a farm. Ultimately, they did some unthinkable things to one another based upon a survival mentality and the 'zero-sum game' mentality. They felt as though others had to die for them to live. In parallel, this is what happens when each of us believes, single-mindedly, in all of our individual positions. Will we too have to determine that people unlike us do not have enough value to live, breathe, or contribute to the world in which we live? This question feels unrealistic, yet it is consistent with how I see people operating every day. We have sunk to an entirely new low in the way we describe the views of our opponents. Our challengers are often described as, "Unbelievably dumb"; "They are doing the worst things that have ever been done"; "They are totally out for themselves"; "Their motives are purely selfish," and so on.

There are two major costs that grow out of counterproductive diversity thinking and conversations: personal costs and societal costs. The personal costs include increased personal ignorance, limited effectiveness in supporting others, and limited personal opportunities. At a larger level, the costs to society include: social ignorance, limited societal effectiveness, economic stagnation, and our society underperforming compared to other countries.

Personal and Societal Ignorance

If people are unwilling to listen to and consider the validity of different points of view, they will remain unaware of those truths that lie outside of their own intellectual grasp. Let's assume you have biases against people who are in the banking industry. There are people who blame the banking industry for many of the economic challenges that currently exist. There are even more people who blame the government for bailing out the banks.

According to an article by David Grant, Congress engaged in a high-stakes game of chicken over raising the national debt limit – something it had done with few controversies some 90 times since 1940. The consensus now is that the fight hurt employment, crushed consumer confidence, caused a major credit-rating agency to downgrade the United States, and according to a recent paper on the impacts of policy uncertainty, hampered overall economic growth for months (Christian Science Monitor, July 5, 2012).

But make no mistake; there are a large number of people in the banking industry who are brilliant about economic matters.

If a person has determined they are not interested in the point of view held by those who are bankers, then they will not benefit from the vast knowledge many of these experts have as it relates to economic matters. Unless each person is committed to becoming an expert at everything, then we must depend on others to help in areas where we may not be as informed. For example, if you look at the strategy most frequently used within cults, they first try to isolate people from their family and the outside world. Their fear is if these converts are able to speak to someone from outside their group, they will learn something that would liberate their minds.

There is also a societal cost related to ignorance. Let's take, for example, the adversarial debates that take place within Congress. It seems fairly obvious to most Americans that neither political party is willing to accept the wise insights that exist among their political opponents. As a result of this stubbornness, the United States' international credit rating was reduced. In other words, as people engage in hostile debates, it sends a message to creditors and credit rating organizations that Americans are incapable of developing joint solutions, which reduces international confidence in our country. As confidence decreases, it also drives up the cost of money. We are fortunate that American bonds remain attractive around the world currently, but our political dysfunction may not allow U.S. bonds to always flourish.

The only thing worse than ignorance itself, is coupling it with confidence. This suggests that not only is the person ignorant, but the individual has a stubborn, or blind commitment to their lack of knowledge. This makes it more difficult to obtain the benefits or information from people who have different points of view. Personal and Societal ignorance also reduces our ability to benefit from synergy. Synergy is an amazing concept demonstrating that 1 + 1 can sometimes equal greater than 2. In other words, people are able to accomplish more together than they can apart. Synergy is also an integral part of success for any team. As a man, I cannot be satisfied receiving benefits when a woman with the same talent, skill and ability does not receive them. I must first be open to listening to those who are knowledgeable regarding these challenges. I must then be willing to join women and other men in breaking down these barriers. As women experience greater equity, all individuals are better equipped to collaborate and deliver better results and solutions to problems in our society. Synergy is the extra value we receive from people working effectively together.

> *"When synergy is not valued, the consequence is a reduction in team effectiveness. This is the cost when people do not respect or value the contributions made by those with opposing points of view."*
>
> - Andy Fishman, Lakota West Teacher and
> Head Varsity Girls Basketball Coach

Limited Effectiveness

Effectiveness is defined as an individual or group activity that is able to fulfill its intended purpose and/or function. A major cost we pay as a result of distorted thinking about diversity is reduced personal and societal effectiveness. If we were to simply look at effectiveness as it relates to the utilization of time, there are two examples that can help us see the cost of personal and societal stubbornness. In the first example, let's say you are the foreman on a construction site. You are responsible for managing a team of five electricians who are in charge of wiring a two-story house for power outlets and light fixtures. You have been given two days to accomplish the task. Out of the five individuals you are supervising, two of them have more years of work experience than you do. At the end of day one, only 25% of the job was complete because of conflicts that arose between you and the two experienced individuals over technical aspects of the job. You had one perspective on how to do the job and they had other perspectives. Although you were the supervisor, they felt strongly they knew more about how to lay out this project than you did. At the end of the day, it doesn't really matter who is right or wrong. If a job is supposed to take two days, at least 50% should be completed by the end of day one. So in this example, you as a supervisor, as well as your team, were unable to accomplish the intended objectives.

In much the same way, school boards have been given the responsibility, authority and control to ensure the proper and effective education of young people in our society. School boards are notorious for becoming social and political footballs that are kicked around by the various interest groups that surround a school community. Parent groups are often divided along cultural and academic interest groups. School activity groups are divided based upon the interest of their specific activity. Teachers, administrators and staff often have very different perspectives of how limited resources should be utilized. So, if school boards are unable to engage those various constituents in meaningful ways, they will be ineffective at accomplishing their vision, mission, goals and objectives. The saddest part about effectiveness is that, all too often, individuals, and organizations are not really measuring it. If effectiveness is not being measured, then there is no real drive to accomplish it. In order for all our American schools to be productive, all the people possessing diverse perspectives should all be sitting at the decision table (school board members, administrators, teachers, students, parents, community members, politicians, and other stakeholders) to determine how to measure school effectiveness. By bringing these various perspectives to the discussion, it will weed out those organizations, or schools, that are ineffective in meeting the needs of customers, or students.

As people engage in daily arguments about differences of opinions, especially regarding topics in which they have a strong emotional connection, it increases the level of destructive stress in their lives. As much as I enjoy listening to talk radio and news, I can literally feel the increased stress and tension I get while listening to people say unkind things to one another. In other words, there is a physical cost related to our counterproductive conversations. When we think the opinions of people who are different from us are unimportant, then we have decided that neither of us will grow based upon the input of others. When we are able to demonstrate respect for different points of view, we establish credibility with diverse individuals. If we lose our ability to influence and support others, we decrease our collective value.

Reduced Personal and Professional Opportunities

People in America have spent a great deal of time arguing about whether or not we should accommodate people in this country who do not speak English. People have the right and freedom to speak whatever language they choose. However, there is no arguing the fact that if you do not speak the dominant culture's language in any country, you will have fewer opportunities. When I work with companies, I strongly encourage them to recruit anybody who has talent, irrespective of their English speaking skills, if the job itself is not dependent on a high level of English proficiency. The ultimate point is that when we don't understand each other, there is a cost we will pay.

Economic Stagnation and Underperformance

When people don't feel respected or included, there is a loss of civility. The summer of 2011 was tagged the, "Arab Spring". There were several countries in the Middle East overtaken by ordinary citizens determined to be valued and create greater opportunities in their country. It reached a breaking point when they decided to protest in the streets and literally overthrow the ruling government, which impeded their local and national economies. Many of us watched television in amazement as the Egyptian people took to the streets while many gave their lives in order to bring about change. The result was a democratic election for the first time in 7,000 years. Even though they were fighting for the right objective, there was a major loss of life and civility for progress to be realized. Unfortunately, we are witnessing a minor loss of civility in America because individuals and groups feel excluded from fair job opportunities. I see this decline as an outgrowth of too many people having resorted to sharing polarizing messages in order to stir up their base to satisfy their political objectives. The United States, certainly, is not experiencing the degree of civil unrest and turmoil the Middle East is experiencing. However, if we do not begin listening to others, our underperforming economic concerns will not improve greatly.

The Benefits of Effective Diversity Conversations

The benefits of effective diversity conversations in many ways are the opposite of the narrow-minded diversity ideas we just discussed.

Increased Knowledge

If $1 + 1 = 2$, then it should be understandable that adding additional perspectives provides you with more information. Every time I listen to someone with whom I have a philosophical or political difference, I learn something I did not previously know. They have been collecting information from different places, where I might not have searched. As I listen to Democrats,

Republicans and Independents, I am confident that all sides have part of the solution to our national debt problems. If they were to spend as much energy collaborating on solutions as they spend attacking each other, there is no doubt we would have already solved the national debt crisis. If you desire more knowledge, one sure way to obtain it is by listening to those who hold opinions that are very different from your own. Even if you simply desire to build stronger arguments for your own point of view, there is significant value gained from spending time studying different perspectives.

Greater Capacity to Identify Best Solutions

A second benefit of welcoming diverse points of view is that there is a greater capacity to identify the best solutions. Too often people are discouraged from listening to diverse points of view. It is as though people are afraid that different perspectives will automatically destroy their original perspective. As people develop openness to diverse viewpoints, there are three specific assets they gain. All input is available for consideration: It is harder to identify the best solutions if you are not willing to consider a wide variety of input. Conversely, your capacity to identify the best solutions increases when you are open to receiving, reviewing, and considering all available information.

There are greater opportunities to identify currently unknown solutions: There is a communication model called Johari's Window which describes four ways personal awareness between individuals impacts their communication effectiveness (Luft, 1950).

Open Self: What I know about myself that others know.
Blind Self: What others know about me, that I don't know.
Hidden Self: What I know and hide from others.
Unknown Self: What others and I don't know about me.

As people collaborate and dialogue with others who have diverse perspectives, they are, collectively, better equipped to identify previously unknown solutions to improve their lives and the lives of others.

Better Equipped to Become One Community

There is a great need across the world to reignite a movement towards unity as fellow human beings. Unity, generally speaking, doesn't grow out of closed-minded conversations. It is shocking to me to hear so many people operating as though it is a crime to consider searching for common ground with those who see the world differently. Negotiators and mediators often begin their work, with activities that help people become better acquainted with each other on a personal level.

Reduce the Drag linked to Diversity Conflict

Most people who know me would not describe me as a person who avoids conflicts. I enjoy vigorously standing up for the things in which I believe. Having said that, there is no doubt that arguments and emotionally-charged debates take a toll on each of us. I was just talking with one of my children before driving to the airport. I was trying to help him understand that badgering and criticizing his siblings was not the best way to get them to change their behavior. In fact, it is almost impossible for any of my children to complete their chores while arguing with a sibling.

Common Language Reduces Social Distance

Periodically, I will invite a colleague to observe one of my training sessions and give me critical feedback. On one occasion, an observer commented he was impressed with my ability to reduce the social distance between participants attending the workshop, and myself. Establishing a common language is one of the tools I use to quickly build a respectful relationship. Negotiations go better with other countries, for example, if you know how to speak their language. One thing that happens to me, most often unconsciously, is I begin to talk like the people I'm talking to. If they have a southern accent, I begin to speak in a similar manner. One of the things that has been discussed, on occasion, is the different ways presidential candidates talk based upon the part of the country they are visiting. Most people do not like it, if they believe you are using an artificial accent in order to gain their support. However, it is very comforting to talk with people who talk like you.

Ultimately, we need to recognize the similarities and differences we have with others and how those differences impact the quality of our conversations. The next three chapters will examine Diversity Conversations with one's self and with those who are similar and dissimilar to us. The final section of the book will explore some of the diversity conflicts we face and strategies that can help us work through these difficult conversations. By the end of the book, you will be a well-informed diversity thought leader because you will have effective tools for navigating these difficult conversations.

Chapter 1 References

Cohen, J. & Davis, R.G.(1991) Third-Person Effects and the Differential Impact in Negative Political Advertising. Journalism and Mass Communication Quarterly, December 1991.

Garramone, Gina M., Atkins, C.K., Pinkleton, B.E, & Cole, R.T. (1990). Effects of negative political advertising on the political process. Journal of Broadcasting & Electronic Media Preview; pages 299-311, Volume 34, Issue 3. Grant, D. (2012) Christian Science Monitor. July 5, 2012. Lau, R.R, Sigelman, L., Heldman, C., & Babbitt, P. (1999). The Effects of Negative Political Advertisements: A Meta-Analytic Assessment. The American Political Science Review American Political Science Association. Vol. 93, No. 4 (Dec., 1999), pp. 851-875.Loden, M., & Rosen, J.B. (1990). Workforce America!: Managing Employee Diversity as a Vital Resource. McGraw-Hill: New York.Luft, J.; Ingham, H. (1950). The Johari window, a graphic model of interpersonal awareness. Proceedings of the western training laboratory in group development (Los Angeles: UCLA).

Diversity Story Chapter 2

"While Talking To Themselves"

In 1991 when I started my consulting firm golf was one of my favorite sports to criticize. While building my house, I decided to walk out back to determine what was behind my house only to discover this amazing golf course. I told my wife I was going to learn to play the game. She enthusiastically agreed. Neither of us had any idea the game had an addictive power much like the street drug crack cocaine. I quickly moved from a casual hacker, to a 5-days a week, driving range regular, tournament playing, buy all the gear, golfer.

Any time I traveled out of town I would take my clubs just in case I had some extra time to play. As I was preparing for a trip to Aiken, S.C., several people warned me this town was not very welcoming to people like me. I didn't give their input much thought as I packed my clubs for the trip.

I arrived in the city, conducted my training class and drove quickly to the nearest golf course in order to get my golf fix in before the sun went down. As I was running to get in my golf cart, the last sound I heard was the Golf Pro saying I probably would only have enough time to play nine holes. I raced around the course but eventually it was too dark to see anything. I ended up having to abandon my cart and walk across a small highway to a nearby restaurant. The thrill of playing golf was over, it was very dark and I was lost. I suddenly began to recall all of the warnings my friends had given me about this town I was visiting.

I had not seen any black people up to this point. But low and behold, as I walked up to this restaurant, I saw this African American female preparing to leave. I was so excited to see her, and felt confident she would be willing to help me get back to my car. I started waving my hands at her as though I knew her and we were best friends. I fully expected her to slow down and at least roll down her window to see what I wanted. She almost ran me over in her rush to leave. So I stood there with my golf clubs on my back and thinking these negative thoughts about her for racing past me. As I stood there staring at the back of her car in disgust, I heard a voice ask me if I needed a ride. I turned around slowly only to see a person who looked like the bad guy in one of those civil rights movies. This new friend of mine was a white gentleman 6'4", in bibbed overalls, a large stomach and a long black beard. He was driving this beat up old Ford pickup truck, with a gun rack on the back, with a big rifle in the rack. It would be a gross understatement to say I was a bit hesitant in my response. I did not answer right away. While I collected my thoughts through a long period of silence, he shared that people are always getting lost on this course and his father played there all the time. His comments increased my confidence that he was not trying to abduct me and I would probably be safe with this unlikely Good Samaritan.

I was constantly talking to myself through every encounter. Often making gross generalizations were opposite of the reality I experienced. This chapter will help us better understand the conversations we have with ourselves.

Chapter

2

Diversity Conversations with Ourselves

"Bringing hidden conversations to the surface"

In our society, people who talk to themselves are seen as a bit unstable. But in fact, everyone has internal conversations with themselves throughout the day. These conversations enable us to navigate between all the choices that are available every moment of our lives. Are we going to take a shower first, or watch the news? Are we going to hit the snooze button on the alarm clock, or get up right away? Are we going to listen silently to a person's point of view or confront them? For me, I am my own best friend and I enjoy the conversations I have with myself each day.

As discussed in the last chapter, I suggest there are three Diversity Conversations. This chapter addresses the first conversation, that is, the conversations we have with ourselves. In this chapter, get ready to bring all your private conversations to the surface so you can learn more about yourself to increase your personal growth. This chapter will also answer the following questions to help you have more effective conversations with yourself:

- What are the diversity conversations we have with ourselves?
- When and where do they occur?
- How can we manage these conversations?
- How do we develop accurate self-awareness?
- What are the barriers to accurate self-awareness?

Diversity Conversations with Ourselves

As we speak to ourselves, it is critical to reflect upon what we are thinking and saying to ourselves. We will discuss mental models later in the book, which are shaped by people and key messages passed on to us in our environment. It is difficult to make diversity progress if we view all our beliefs as true and irrefutable. Therefore, we must learn to recognize that some ideas we believe may simply be wrong.

In order to sustain healthy conversations with people who have diverse points of view, several key points are needed. First, and foremost, all of the information we have about diverse people and their points of views are not accurate. In my workshops, a question I always ask participants is, "How many of you have ever been confident that you knew something to be true only to discover you were wrong?" Virtually everyone expresses having had that experience.

Personally, there is nothing that bothers me more than being confidently wrong about something. This tends to happen frequently in many marriages, including my own. My wife has been, by far, my greatest teacher, while I have been her most difficult student. I readily admit to being a slow, albeit grateful, learner. When I first got married, I remember saying to my wife, "You are so lucky to be married to me because I am the easiest guy in the world to get along with." I was so confident she would discover this to be the truth. Additionally, nothing in my first 28 years of living suggested this statement was not 100% accurate. Unfortunately, I had very little experience in long term dating prior to meeting my wife. So in my mind, things were pretty easy. I saw myself as carefree, flexible, and open to make adjustments based on my wife's interests and needs. But after 23 years of marriage, with my wife as my mirror, her feedback has convinced me I did not have a clue about marriage. Marriage has provided me with some of life's most important lessons about diversity as well. If people make room for the fact that what we think, feel, or believe to be true might actually be false, then maybe we can reduce the bitter conflicts that arise so often in conversations about diversity.

It is hard to resolve conflicts if you always believe you are right and your opponents are wrong. One might ask, "What is the value of considering that my position in a diversity argument could be wrong?" My answer is that it allows you to make some space in your mind for the validity of different points of view. This is not suggesting that you eliminate what you think is right, but do not hold on so strongly to the infallibility of your thoughts.

Just recently, my assistant developed a system for ensuring that all of my important phone messages were available to me on the calendar of my Smartphone. In my private conversation with myself, I was never quite pleased with this new process as I wanted to be able to ask her daily for numbers. However, I decided to give in to her system, like any good boss. One day I needed to make an important call so I looked on my phone calendar, but I found it was completely empty. I quickly reflected back on this new system and my assistant mentioning how this new process would save time. With confidence, and maybe even a twinge of indignation, I called her to my office to make the point that she was not following through on the systems she created and loved. She came into my office and I showed her my empty phone calendar. Immediately, she looked at the calendar on her computer; all of the information was there. By the time she returned to tell me that all of the information was on our common calendar, I remembered I had recently visited the Apple Store and received a new iPhone. Yet, I had not taken the opportunity to sync it with our calendar. Needless to say, I ate crow that day. The point is, even though I was completely confident in my own mind, I was embarrassingly wrong. In other words, we must reflect on the conversations we are having with ourselves. We must first understand how our point of view was developed and then be prepared to understand that no matter how confident we are about something, we could be wrong.

When and Where do these Conversations Occur?

Most people have the good fortune of being their own best friend. We literally have inner conversations with ourselves throughout the day. Some might suggest the conversation continue even while we are sleeping.

When we are having discussions within ourselves on diversity-related matters, most people start with their own personal beliefs. In short, our belief systems have been established over a lifetime and they are very valuable tools. Our belief system also gives us a sense of security and helps us to remain comfortable in the choices we make. Our internal conversations help us evaluate new information in order to determine how it aligns with our beliefs. For most people, information that is consistent with their belief systems is more readily received than information that may be inconsistent with their beliefs.

If you were in a big music superstore and you loved country music, it probably would be safe to bet if you had to pick out twenty free CD's, the majority would be country as opposed to pop, hip hop, or another genre of music. In other words, we generally go through life collecting information that is consistent with our personal tastes and ultimately our beliefs. Generally speaking, people read and listen more to the people and information that is most closely aligned with their own perspective. Also, people generally collect information to build up their side of an argument and refute those perspectives with which they disagree. It is rare for people to receive new information without reacting to it and allowing the content to stand on its own.

It doesn't take very long for the average person to listen to a speaker, a newscast, or a radio program to determine if the information is consistent with their personal point of view. This creates a significant challenge for us as it relates to managing diversity conversations. If 90% of a person's effort is spent on maintaining their current belief systems, then it becomes very difficult for people to learn anything new. Developing and maintaining belief systems provides people with a sense of comfort, familiarity and consistency in the world. But, integrating different information and new beliefs is a very unsettling experience for most. Thus, the reward we receive for incorporating new and different points of view, is a broader perspective of the world around us and an increased ability to more effectively correct inaccurate internal conversations.

In order to manage our internal conversations, we must also begin by recognizing the high degree of loyalty we have to our current belief system. As already stated, it is difficult to accept new or unfamiliar information. Therefore, it is imperative we force ourselves to listen to and seek to understand information that is different. Surprisingly, we may find ourselves battling our own internal voice, or beliefs, if we are to ever embrace truth that may be inconsistent with our current belief systems. The only thing that is powerful enough to justify an investment of this kind of energy is the potential we may discover a truth we were historically not aware of prior to the new knowledge. In other words, the reason that we must battle ourselves is to avoid the high cost we pay as individuals and as a society for our cultural blind spots.

Of course, it is much harder to implement this strategy than it is to simply discuss it. Once belief systems are firmly established, people generally spend a great deal of energy defending them. When you collect enough life experiences in being confidently wrong, it forces you to become less stubborn and more open to opposing points of views.

When we have conversations with ourselves, they are private conversations. We do not have to be as guarded as we are when talking to others. This small, but important fact should provide a greater amount of latitude to be more honest with ourselves regarding what we truly believe about a person or situation. No one else has to ever know what we feel, think or believe. Let me provide a real life example that illustrates this point. Recently, there was a white supremacist interviewed on the evening news. He was making comments about the significance of white people and the importance of them recognizing the value of supporting political agendas that are in their best interest. Looking at the situation I just experienced while sitting on the couch, here is what I recall:

1. The news station has already defined the speaker as a white supremacist.
2. I am an African-American.

3. I am a diversity consultant.

4. As an African-American diversity consultant, I am expected to oppose the viewpoint of a self-described white supremacist.

5. In the privacy of my own head, I get to explore if I think there is any validity to the points he made.

I do not have to dismiss his viewpoint immediately based on anyone else's perspective. The conversations we have in our heads are like skinny-dipping in our own pool with a privacy fence. You are free to be you and it does not really matter what other people think. So while I was listening to this particular individual, I was free to determine what I thought about what he was saying. I looked at his facial expression. I listened to the tone of his voice and the message he was delivering. I came to conclude he was a fairly rational thinker and the title "white supremacist" didn't seem to fit the person I was observing on television. I also felt as though there was some validity to the viewpoint he was sharing. I, Eric Ellis, the African-American Diversity Consultant, agreed with the self-described white supremacist that said it is important for people to consider supporting what might be in their best interest. "Oh No!! What's the world coming to?" I thought.

I, like most people, spend the majority of my time and energy studying information that is consistent with what I believe. While I think it is beneficial to have belief systems and to collect information that reinforces your beliefs; it is also a good practice to collect information that may be opposed to your philosophical views. In essence, it is necessary and crucial to maintain openness to information that is different from what we believe.

How to Develop Accurate Self-Awareness

According to business expert Daniel Goleman, 90% of the competencies necessary to be a successful leader and deliver superior performance are social and emotional in nature (Goleman, 1998). Furthermore, effective people skills are twice as important as technical expertise and IQ combined. This is why some very smart people who lack sensitivity fail. Self-awareness is one of the most important keys to effective communication with people who are different from you. Those individuals who have an accurate view of themselves are better equipped to monitor their thoughts and behaviors in order to make appropriate adjustments to create healthier discussions with others who are different. The lack of self-awareness ranks as one of the most frequent characteristics of a person ineffective in relating with others.

Self-awareness is closely linked with emotional intelligence, which is the capacity for recognizing our own feelings and those of others, for motivating ourselves, and for managing emotions. There is no place that accurate self-awareness is more difficult to achieve than in the area of diversity. Barriers to accurate self-awareness and strategies for improving self-awareness are critical to having effective conversations with yourself.

In order to reflect on accurate self-awareness, we must define accurate self-awareness and discuss strategies for becoming more self-aware. We must recognize our "Framework of Denial," along with the characteristics of people who are highly self-aware and those who are not. Finally, strategies for improving your own self-awareness skills are recommended.

Accurate Self-Awareness

Accurate self-awareness is the ability to honestly recognize one's strengths and weaknesses in the area of diversity and human understanding. It is the ability to effectively read how we react to cues in the environment and to be aware of how our emotions and mental models affect our ability to relate to others who are different. It is also the desire to receive feedback and the willingness to engage in continuous learning and self-development. In the area of diversity and human understanding, it is imperative to understand the three dimensions of Diversity Conversations, especially the conversation with yourself. Having this understanding will help you be more effective at having conversations with like others and those who are unlike you, which will be discussed more in Chapters 3 and 4.

Framework of Denial

There are several barriers that impact people's willingness to admit their personal biases. I describe these barriers as the "Framework of Denial." This concept includes things that cause people to be dishonest regarding their personal prejudices and biases toward others. The following are common elements of this framework:

Key Realities of Framework of Denial

- There is a social benefit gained from being perceived as fair and open.
- Discrimination is not viewed as desirable behavior.

- There is no perceived social benefit from admitting personal prejudices.
- There are penalties for people who offend others or display their personal prejudices.
- People are often comfortable with the incongruence that exists between their private beliefs and public declarations.

There is a social benefit gained from being perceived as fair and open. One of the major tenets of the U.S. Declaration of Independence is that all men are created equal. Because this concept plays such a key role in ensuring the American lifestyle, it is generally believed that complying, at least outwardly, with this ideal makes someone more patriotic or "American." There are many examples that support the assertion that people want to be perceived as fair and open. In the 1990s, ABC Television conducted several news reports on discrimination using hidden cameras. In cases when the hidden camera had uncovered discriminatory treatment based on age, gender, race, and weight, the discriminator was questioned regarding their behavior. Every person accused of discriminatory behavior denied having any underlying prejudices that led to their unfair behavior. Even though the person had clearly performed discriminatory actions, they believed they would be punished for openly admitting their prejudices. In most cases, they made excuses for their actions, became angry, and refused to discuss the situation.

Discrimination Defined

Webster's Dictionary defines discrimination as the act of discriminating, the process by which two stimuli differing in some aspect are responded to differently, the quality or power of finely distinguishing, the act, practice, or an instance of discriminating categorically rather than individually, prejudiced or prejudicial outlook, action, or treatment like racial discrimination. When we discuss the negative type of human discrimination, most people would publicly agree that human discrimination is not a good thing. Much of the progress made during the 1960's Civil Rights movement did a lot to convince our nation that discrimination was an indefensible moral stance. Once discrimination gained a negative connotation, it became much more difficult for the average person to admit he discriminates on a regular basis. People often get angry at the notion that someone would accuse them of being discriminatory, but the truth is most people regularly discriminate against others. Because discrimination is viewed as bad behavior, people often deceive themselves due to a subconscious reflex that says, "I'm not that bad person who would treat others unfairly." We know discrimination is wrong; but we end up deceiving ourselves regarding our own behavior in order to avoid facing an uncomfortable truth.

No Social Benefits for Admitting Personal Prejudices

Unfortunately, there are not many perceived benefits gained from admitting personal prejudices. Since there are so few benefits to being honest about our shortcomings, it is no wonder so few people admit they have them. One of the greatest contributors to an individual denying their prejudices is viewing themselves as culturally enlightened. I coined a term, "The Arrogance of the Enlightened," to describe the attitude and behavior of those who consider themselves to be open and without bias. This group of people generally view themselves as having arrived at "Diversity Heaven." They know all the right answers and their job is to fix all the other broken people in society. The term arrogance is used because these people are typically not open to feedback regarding their ineffective approaches to educating others. Enlightened refers to the way they see themselves as opposed to their true state of diversity enlightenment. Some of these people have historically been discriminated against. Others may just consider themselves social liberals. This term is aimed at disarming the attitude that causes some people to judge others as ignorant, while acting as though they themselves have no need for further growth. This term also describes a factor that causes some members of the dominant culture to avoid scrutinizing their shortcomings regarding discrimination and bias.

The Penalties for Offending Others

One major contributor to the Framework of Denial is the potential for punishment, or the real penalties people can receive from offending others or displaying their personal prejudices. Generally, people notice when famous people are penalized for making comments that are deemed offensive to others. People have also heard of or known someone in their work environment, or another organization, who was penalized for saying something offensive about others. Individuals have been personally reprimanded and companies have lost millions of dollars as a result of offensive comments used in the workplace. Some companies who have experienced financial penalties for offensive comments are:

- U.S. Government, $550 Million suit on Gender Discrimination
- Mitsubishi, $34 Million on Gender Suits
- Texaco, $176 Million settlement on Racial Bias
- Shoney's, $134 Million settlement on Racial Discrimination

Characteristics of People Highly Self-Aware:

People who are highly self-aware often display the following characteristics: Their personal view of themselves lines up with the way others see them. They are able to articulate their prejudices first to themselves and then to others. They are accepting of feedback and often seek it out. Whereas, people who are not highly self-aware see themselves more positively than do others around them. They are not able to articulate their shortcomings and they reject feedback that accurately describes them.

Strategies to Improve Accurate Self-Awareness

There are some specific strategies for improving your accurate self-awareness. Here are four steps you can take to improve your self-awareness:

- Engage in Regular Self- Analysis
- Develop a Process for Gaining Regular Feedback
- Personal Feedback Coaches
- Develop Intellectual Curiosity

Engage in Regular Self-Analysis

Introspection is a very healthy activity. In order to improve our ability to be accurately self-aware, we must first start by studying ourselves. This often means consciously reviewing what we believe are our strengths, weaknesses, thoughts, reactions, and mental models regarding human differences.

Let me provide a personal example: I like people, so I seek to put people at ease in conversations. I also study the body language of others to check their receptivity to my perspective. Consequently, I actively listen and often paraphrase what people say to me. However, I am also opinionated and find it difficult to be politically correct. It is also hard for me to pay attention over long periods of time. The ancient Temple of Apollo in Delphi, Greece has the maxim, "Know thyself" inscribed on it. This maxim reinforces the fact that it is important for people to have an accurate understanding of themselves. As stated earlier in the chapter, others do not know all of our weaknesses, character flaws and shortcomings. However, we must be conscious of our own strengths and weaknesses and be prepared to work on them, continuously, in order to be better citizens in our communities.

Develop a Process for Receiving Continuous Feedback

One of the best strategies for increasing accurate self-awareness is to use a formal tool to learn more about yourself. Instruments like DISC, Myers Briggs Type Indicator, Harvard Implicit Association Test (IAT), and other similar tools can provide an individual with a wealth of knowledge about himself based on a self-report. It is also possible to use one of the many 360-degree feedback tools. These tools are valuable as a way of getting formal feedback from people who interact with others in a work environment.

Personal Feedback Coaches

Everyone can benefit from having people in your life who can provide you with an honest assessment of yourself and how you are impacting others. My wife has been my main source of positive and constructive feedback. I often joke with her and say, "Everyone I dated before I married you said I was the nicest, sweetest, most considerate person they had ever met, and then I got married." She quickly replies by saying two things: "First of all, people always lie to people during the dating process, and secondly, no one ever loved you like I do." If you choose to use a feedback coach, make sure it is someone who will be honest with you about what he or she observes in your behavior. Also make sure your coach is someone from whom you can objectively receive both praise and criticism.

Take Time to Study Environmental Cues

In order to improve accurate self-awareness, an individual must take time to study his or her environment. We must focus on what we say, how we talk to others, and how others are reacting to who we are, what we look like, and what we are saying. Whatever system you develop, the important thing is to identify a consistent way of gaining ongoing feedback from others. Know your biases, mental models, prejudices, hot buttons, squishy spots, values, strengths, and limitations.

Develop Intellectual Curiosity

As people work to develop their skills at communicating effectively with people who are different, it is helpful to adapt a philosophy of intellectual curiosity. Intellectual curiosity is defined as a desire to explore perspectives that are both similar and different from your own. These questions should be asked as you cultivate your intellectual curiosity:

1. What causes you to develop intellectual curiosity?
2. What causes you to avoid exploring perspectives from other people's point of view?
3. Why is being intellectually curious important to you?
4. How can you develop and implement intellectual

Intellectual Curiosity?

People who are intellectually curious have a thirst for learning about points of view held by others. It is important to recognize that as people gain greater insight into what others think and believe, their own understanding of a subject and the world is improved.

What causes people to develop intellectual curiosity?

Intellectual curiosity is something we have naturally. At age two, a child begins to experiment with the world. By the age of three, a child's mind is open to all sorts of information. My children used to say they were "experimenting," when they set a newspaper on fire or put a fork in an electrical outlet, but we did not always take quite as academic a view of their intellectual curiosity. Nevertheless, intellectual curiosity was what it was; they were exploring their boundaries. By age 13, most children have begun to zero in on their specific talents based on the skills they have developed. As adults, although more difficult, it is not impossible to reinvigorate this curiosity.

Why reject perspectives from other peoples' point of view?

Often when people are not confident in their own point of view, they are hesitant to listen to other points of view. People also fear other perspectives because a different perspective may make more sense than what they believe. They fear having to admit they are incorrect about a position they hold. Finally, research suggests that people value predictability and stability, so it is very uncomfortable for the average person to change his or her point of view, even if other perspectives are more accurate.

Why is being intellectually curious important?

Intellectual curiosity is important because it creates an appetite for learning. By definition, it suggests we are willing to entertain other points of view. Intellectual curiosity can be a lifetime occupation. As people remain curious, they are better equipped to discover the truth. Over the years, I have reduced my loyalty to groups and increased my allegiance to what is true, or what is right. I often say that truth does not belong to any one particular group. Sometimes conservatives have the truth on an issue, and sometimes liberals have the truth. Sometimes men have the truth on an issue, and in other situations, women have a perspective that is more valuable. The truth tends to be like a moving target. Therefore, we need to align ourselves with the truth according to our understanding instead of aligning ourselves with a group of people with whom we have certain characteristics in common.

Strategies to Develop and Implement Intellectual Curiosity

In closing out this chapter, here are some strategies for developing and implementing an intellectual curiosity to cultivate conversations with yourself:

- Seek to understand points of view that differ from your own.
- Maintain an ability to validate aspects of perspectives that differ from your own.
- Seek to align yourself with truth versus cultural and political points of view.

- Recognize that each of us has internal conversations.
- Recognize that you have collected information on people and institutions in your environment.
- Recognize your prejudices, biases, and hot buttons and how they influence your thinking.
- Ask, "what might I be missing as I think about diverse people or points of view?"

Now that you better understand diversity conversations with yourself and how to improve your self-awareness, the next two chapters cover having conversations with those like you and having conversations with people who are very different from you. Each of these principles builds upon the foundation of having conversations with yourself in the three dimensions of diversity conversations.

References: ABC News, Goleman, D. (1998), Webster's Dictionary

Diversity Story Chapter 3

"Challenging Situations Require Patience"

On April 7, 2001, officers within The Cincinnati Police Department shot and fatally killed Timothy Thomas, an unarmed 19 year old African American. A peaceful protest turned violent on April 9th, which triggered several days of civil unrest in the Over-the-Rhine area of Cincinnati, Ohio. I had been in business for ten years at this point and felt great compassion and concern for my city. There were many people trying to figure out what we needed to do in order to bring calm to this nationally-televised, citywide tragedy.

Our community was sharply divided between those who felt as though this unrest was long overdue. Some believed that when the systems of equity and justice operate in ways that are measurably unfair, some people would seek justice by any means necessary. However, there were others who felt strongly that the violence had nothing to do with social or economic injustice. They felt the "riots" were completely wrong, as though it was simply criminal activity. They also believed that anyone who believed there was justification for these activities was just as misguided as those who caused the destruction of property.

For anyone committed to fairness, equity, and respect, there was plenty of work to do during this period. There were three specific roles I played: 1) an unofficial leadership negotiator, 2) facilitator for neighborhood focus group meetings, and 3) initiator of a citywide television program to bring about community healing and understanding.

There were two men who were viewed as representing the major voices on each side of this conflict: Charlie Luken (former Cincinnati Mayor) and Rev. Dr. Damon Lynch III, a local pastor and community leader. I knew both of these men and met with each of them separately in order to determine how we could create a pathway forward for the people in our city. After meeting with each of them, I very quickly realized they believed so strongly in their positions that it was unlikely progress was going to be made if it was dependent upon their finding common ground. Each leader had a legitimate point of view and was unwilling to be viewed as weak by their constituents for meeting with the other side. I was not very successful in bringing them together.

The second role I played was facilitator of the first community meeting to identify the issues and concerns that may have led to the civil unrest in the community. We met in the community of Avondale at the Urban League building. There were about 500 people in attendance. People lined up to give their perspective along with suggestions for how we could move forward as a community. This was an extremely civil and productive conversation. There were only a couple of people who were disruptive, but I had support from the Nation of Islam brothers who were there to help us keep the peace.

The third role I played was host and co-creator of a television program called *"Common Ground"*. This program was created as a way of expanding our dialogue to the entire Cincinnati community. We developed a first ever community-wide discussion on Diversity through a local media simulcast program. There was a lot of local and national attention on what we were attempting to do.

Overall, we were not very successful in the short-term. It became painfully clear that our diverse community didn't seem to have a real strong desire to ease the tension through collaboration and compromise. Long-term, however, positive strides were made in opening up a productive dialogue on strategies to resolve some of our equity and justice issues.

Chapter

3

Diversity Conversations with Like Others

"Birds of the same feather"

People often ask, "Why don't we focus more on our similarities?" This chapter will explore the conversations we have with people like ourselves. These conversations are very important. There are several key questions we will review: How are people similar? Why are similarities important? And, why don't people talk more about similarities? We will then explore practical ways of navigating conversations with people like ourselves.

How are people similar?

You have heard the saying, "Birds of a feather flock together." This cliché tends to be true. It does not take long to see this truth if you go into the cafeteria of any diverse high school in America. You will find young people clustered together with those who are like them. Whether that similarity is based upon their race, ethnicity, or their affiliation in music or sports, there is something comforting about people associating with others who are like themselves.

Abraham Maslow is known as one of the world's most renowned psychologists. In 1943, he developed "Maslow's Hierarchy of Needs." Maslow's theory describes people as having five fundamental needs. The first need is physiological: breathing, food, water, sex, sleep, and excretion. The next level of Maslow's hierarchy is safety and security through employment, resources, morality, family, health, and property. The third level is love and belonging. This includes a need for freedom, family, and intimacy. The fourth hierarchy is the need for esteem. This level includes self-esteem, achievement, respect for others, and being respected by others. The highest level of Maslow's needs is self-actualization. That is, realizing personal potential, creativity, spontaneity, problem solving, lack of prejudice, and acceptance of facts (Maslow, 1943).

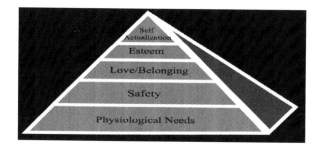

Figure 3.1: Maslow's Hierarchy of Needs

According to Maslow, once you have mastered all these levels, you are equipped to transcend to assist others in reaching your level.

Maslow's theory sought to explain what motivates human beings. His research identified that people are driven to meet their most basic needs first. As those needs are met, people then focus on higher needs, with the goal of reaching self-actualization. In short, before an individual can think about being the president, he must eat. It is important for us to understand that people are basically influenced by many of the same needs. This also explains some of the difficulties people may have valuing diverse perspectives, especially if some of their lower-level needs are not being met.

It is important that people spend time with others who look like them, talk like them, think, and act like them. Beyond enjoying this time together, having conversations with like others generates self-affirmation that is beneficial for both parties.

I had the opportunity on a couple of occasions, to witness this as an outsider, while in the company of like others. I was asked to be a keynote speaker at a women's empowerment conference. As a diversity consultant, I have spent a great deal of time studying various issues that have impacted women and their ability to receive fair and equitable treatment in the workplace. As I was preparing my speech, I was quite comfortable I had a message that could be helpful for those in attendance. But, I did not anticipate the difficulty I would face by simply attending the conference. When I showed up at the convention center, an ambassador for the conference greeted me and said, "You must be our speaker." She escorted me to where I was to speak and asked if I needed anything for the speech. When I told her I was fine, she invited me to the networking reception in Ballroom C. This sounded like a good idea, so I quickly set up my PowerPoint presentation and went to their reception in anticipation of meeting some of the people who would be in my audience. I was not fully prepared for the feelings I experienced however, as I walked into the ballroom filled with hundreds of women and no men. The feeling I had was of complete and utter anxiety. I had no idea how uncomfortable I would feel as the only man in the room. Women made comments to me like, "Who let you in here?" "Are you going to be serving us lunch?" "Hey girls, look it's a man!" Each of those comments, taken individually, may not seem like much, but collectively, they began to wear me down. I felt like I was going from one group to another as an unwelcomed guest at a party of best friends. My main objective was to remove myself from this uncomfortable situation. As an extrovert, surprisingly, I left the room as though I had somewhere important to go, or had an important call to take. Outside the ballroom, the restroom became my temporary hideout and refuge.

This experience stood in stark contrast to another conference I attended where I was speaking to a group of minority business owners. Many of them were friends I knew. As I came into the room, several men and women warmly greeted me with hugs and affirmation. Several asked how my family was doing. Stated simply, I was completely at ease and comfortable with others like myself.

People Who Look Like Us

In the animal kingdom, it is not uncommon to see interactions between animals that are alike. Among human beings, we see a similar pattern. People choose to date or marry those who have a similar level of attractiveness. On occasion, I have been bold enough to say, "Hey, you guys match!" In other words, you look like a fit. Why does this occur? Why do people choose to date people who are viewed as being on the same level, or even of their same race?

A part of this answer clearly has been determined by how we were raised and socialized. It also comes from prejudices and biases we have inherited from family, friends, and the environments where we have lived. It is widely accepted that people typically choose to connect with others who look like them. Take a moment to think about entering a room with four different groups. One group is women from China; another is a Nigerian group of men and women dressed in their cultural outfits; another group is Middle Eastern men; while a final group is men and women of different ages of your same ethnic and racial background. Which group would you tend to gravitate towards and why? Unless you had a pre-existing relationship with someone in the different cultural groups, I suggest you would be drawn to those who look most like you.

People Who Talk like Us

When you grow up in a particular part of the country, one of the gifts you typically receive is an accent or dialect similar to others who live in that particular area. My family has small farming town roots. When my father attended college, they called him "country boy" because he spoke with the dialect of the farming families in his hometown. Many of us connect with people more easily if they speak like we do and use the same dialect. Many times, the greatest barrier that separates people is the lack of a common language.

A common language has an ability to tear down the walls of human separation. From a global perspective, negotiations are more effective with other countries if a common language is spoken. People have spent a great deal of energy debating whether or not it is wise for political candidates to alter their natural dialect to conform to the linguistic styles of their diverse audiences. Some argue these adjustments represent the worst kind of political pandering. On the other hand, there are linguistic experts who adamantly disagree. They describe these kinds of cultural adjustments as respectful of the groups the candidates are addressing. It has been suggested these adjustments may even be unconscious (CNN "Debate Night in America" 10-3-12). I work very hard during training sessions to reduce the social distance between the workshop participants and myself. Common language has the ability to bring people together.

Why are Similarities Important?

As I travel conducting leadership retreats, it is quite common for me to identify the local golf courses before I arrive. Generally speaking, I do most of my traveling alone. So if I play golf, it is either unaccompanied, with friends or with people whom I have never met before. Most of the time, playing golf with random strangers is generally fun, especially if they are decent players. On some occasions, I get paired up with someone with whom the chemistry is not the best.

Such was the case when I traveled to Athens, Georgia on a beautiful afternoon. There was no wind, so I imagined driving the ball 300 yards down the middle of the fairway. I rushed to the course to play nine holes of golf, after a speaking engagement. When I arrived at the pro-shop, they let me know single golfers were not encouraged, so they invited me to join a twosome that was preparing to play. Being a gregarious person, I was excited about meeting new people. So I drove my cart up to hole number one. There were two older, white-haired gentlemen at the first tee box. They did not notice me, so I introduced myself. "Hey guys, they asked me to join your twosome," I said. The one with the longest, whitest beard turned around and said, "You must be from the north." My mind began to quickly surmise that, maybe, I should ask to be paired with another group. But I persevered and worked to salvage what looked to be a bad round in the making. I responded with the greatest amount of respect I could muster, "Yes sir, I am! I'm here from Cincinnati, Ohio." To that he responded, "I'm so sick of northerners coming to the south and messing this place up." To which I gave no response.

Clearly, there were several options available to me as to how to respond. I have been known to "fight fire with fire." However, on this particular day, I was willing to just ignore the insults and focus on playing golf. In my mind, I figured this was going to be a very long and quiet round of golf. The two gentlemen got up to the first tee box. The first one hit his ball about 100 yards and into the trees on the left side of the fairway. Then, his white-bearded friend got up and hit his ball into the woods on the right side. So, now it was my turn. I teed up my ball and prayed I would hit the ball well. I surely did and hit the ball 290 yards, right down the middle of the fairway.

We drove our carts in silence to the next tee, but make no mistake, they had noticed the quality of my golf shot. The next two or three holes repeated a similar pattern. By the fourth hole, one of the gentlemen made the second comment of the day and said, "Hey, I feel like I'm playing with Tiger Woods." Now, there are some African-American golfers who would have been offended by the comment. But, I viewed it as an upgrade from where we had been. I thanked him for the compliment and thought we might be making progress. After a couple more holes, the ice was broken, their guards were down, and we began to transcend the things that made us different. We came together on the common ground of being golf enthusiasts. By the time we ended the round, the bearded gentleman, who had initially made the comment about the north, was inviting me over to his house for dinner. The point of the story is when people have something in common, they can overcome whatever differences may exist.

Why don't People Talk More about Similarities?

Typically speaking, people don't just sit around saying, "Let's talk about our similarities." It just happens. Almost subconsciously, we enjoy sharing with individuals who like the things we like. It is refreshing when you start a sentence and someone else can finish it because they understand and can relate to a subject of interest. We know that advertising strategies are often built to attract a particular target population. Information is often easier to receive, if it is consistent with your values and beliefs. We know that facial expressions register more calm and enjoyment when they are listening to something with which they agree. The problem we face in America is that as people spend a majority of their time listening to information that reinforces their general beliefs, they are less capable of recognizing the value of opposing points of view. Believe it or not, I have had people ask in workshops, "Why don't we have classes focused on our similarities?" As a researcher, business consultant, and executive coach, I know you cannot lead an effective diversity seminar without significant conversation about what people have in common.

Managing Diversity Conversations with People Like Ourselves

These conversations probably occur more often than conversations with people who are different from us. There are three types of conversations we can engage in when we talk to people like ourselves. They are: 1) conversations of agreement, 2) conversations of challenge and, 3) conversations of questioning (ACQ). We will explore each conversation's value and consider possible objectives you may want to consider as you engage in these discussions. Even when we are speaking with people similar to ourselves, we can still achieve progress on diversity. We can discuss things with which we agree, we can challenge each other on our commonly held beliefs, or we can identify questions we have regarding the things we believe.

Conversations of Agreement

We absolutely have to talk to people who see diversity issues like we see them. It is comforting for our values and beliefs to be affirmed by others. But, diversity is often difficult to talk about. People feel there is a risk in speaking openly and frankly about what they believe. So, when you are speaking to people who are like you about diversity topics, where there is agreement, there is a sense of relief.

Conversations of Challenge

In order for significant growth to take place regarding diversity, individuals must challenge others within their group to make some adjustments in their belief systems. Whether it is a personal, political, or social belief, it is never easy to challenge people within your own group. When you are a member of a minority group, you have, most likely, experienced prejudice and discrimination. Therefore, these experiences make it very easy to remain silent when members of your group are falsely blaming others for their problems. If we are going to have an honest conversation, there are a few realities we must admit. First, that discrimination is real and occurs on a regular basis. Secondly, institutional prejudice will not end without the pressure of vigilant leaders and activists. Finally, it is irresponsible for leaders to suggest that a group of people cannot succeed unless another group comes to rescue them. I believe one of the important roles we play within our own cultural group is that of challenging some of the philosophies we commonly share.

Conversations of Questioning

Human beings are never very comfortable with uncertainty. I would suggest there is value in responding to certain diversity issues with a question. For example, let's say I am a member of the National Rifle Association. Let us assume my friend and I have hunted together for 20 years and we have attended gun rallies for the last 15 years about the importance of maintaining our freedom to bear arms. What typically happens is there is an established set of principles and beliefs we embrace in order to be a part of the group. Now let's say my beliefs evolved when I watched the local news story stating that several young people have been accidently shot because of guns being available in the home. I then begin to question and perhaps change my original belief. My point here is that there is value in saying to others who are like you, "I'm not sure I still believe in the position we have held." In other words, you do not have to agree or challenge; sometimes it is simply helpful to question a commonly held point of view. .

References: Maslow, A.H. (1943). "A Theory of Human Motivation," Psychological Review 50(4): 370-96.

Diversity Story Chapter 4

"The Truth According To Your Understanding"

There is a wonderful, diverse, non-denominational church in Ohio. If you ever met the Pastor, you would think his smile and laugh were simply infectious. Many people often asked how a small-town country cowboy and horse trader could ever build a multi-million dollar church with one of the most diverse congregations in the country. He would say, "God did it."

I attended the church for many years and enjoyed the fiery preaching, powerful choir, and most of all, the people. The Pastor and his wife were very passionate about their beliefs, and I found the Pastor's honesty very refreshing. He did something I've only seen a very few leaders do, he honestly shared his political convictions. On the surface, one might say, that doesn't seem rare, or difficult at all. I would suggest it is extremely rare among leaders of very diverse congregations. The Pastors are sensitive to the fact that their members are politically diverse. They often don't want to risk alienating anyone, or put their tax exempt status in jeopardy. What impressed me the most was his willingness to possibly lose people and financial support in order to share what he believed was the truth.

In order to engage in meaningful conversations with people who view the world differently, it is important to understand the motives that are influencing their decisions. I feel strongly that people should remain loyal to the truth, according to their understanding. When your level of understanding changes, it is important for you to change. Unfortunately, we refer to people who change their minds as flip floppers, which doesn't encourage many people to take this pathway.

Chapter

4

Diversity Conversations with Diverse

Others

*"Everyone we meet has some things in common
and other things that differ"*

My very first memories as a child were growing up in the inner city
of Dayton, Ohio in the 1960's. My parents kept my siblings and me
very busy with chores and other activities in order to reduce the
time we had to argue and fight. On a typical evening, the kitchen
was our family gathering place. We loved to debate on any topic
until someone yelled, "Dr. King's on TV!" We would immediately
make a mad dash to the living room so we could hear what Dr.
King had to say. Unfortunately, if you were the last one in the
living room, you inevitably were given the task of holding the
television antenna in order to improve the reception. The
television's audio quality was better than the video, so you could
hear Dr. King, even if you could not see him on the screen very
well. As important as Dr. King was, another sound that was even
more beloved was the neighborhood ice cream truck driving down
the street. No matter who was talking, or what we were doing, it all
became irrelevant once we heard the truck's very familiar song. My

mother could get us to do anything for the seventy-five cents needed to get an ice cream sandwich or cone. I do not think we would have been as energized if the ice cream man sold only one flavor. The fact that you could choose vanilla, strawberry, or chocolate flavors, a drumstick, or a banana split increased our overall excitement.

Ice cream is very insignificant in comparison to people. Nonetheless, we are a more exciting society because of our diversity. Anthropologists have suggested that people are biologically 99.6% the same (Sagan). They have suggested that we, in many ways, are all a part of one race, the human race. So why do we have so much conflict based upon our skin tone, our gender, or our socioeconomic status?

Over the 25 years I have spent conducting diversity workshops, it almost never fails that a participant will say, "I think we should just see people as people." Others around the room often nod their heads in agreement. In so many ways, I want to agree with their point of view. Then, that idealistic view gets run over by the hundreds of stories people share in our classes about being ostracized or victimized because of the fact they were different from those who chose to harass them.

There are several key questions that will be explored and answered in this chapter. We will reflect on our personal backgrounds, how we define bias, and the four types of biases. We will also discuss how prejudice and discrimination are differentiated; how we are socialized regarding our human differences and the importance of de-stigmatizing prejudice so people can affiliate with their personal biases. Finally, the chapter will close by offering a practical tool to reduce conflict with diverse others.

To begin this chapter, I would like to walk you through my family background. As you spend time in my home with my family of origin, I believe you will be able to identify experiences in your own upbringing that have resulted in your own personal bias.

My Family

Like you, my family has always been very important to me. My father was born and raised on a farm. He had 12 brothers and sisters and his father had a third grade education. I will always remember the stories my father told me about growing up on the farm. Their family lived in Cayuga, Illinois, a small, country town about three hours south of Chicago. Being a light-skinned man, my grandfather was given 300 acres of land to sharecrop because they thought he was white. It was not until Grandpa Ellis brought his black wife and 12 children to this little town that people realized he was a black man. My father spoke often about the people who lived in his community.

Although my family faced cultural and racial conflicts at the beginning, eventually they established very strong bonds with people in their community. Ultimately, the character and work ethic of my family enabled them to build strong relationships with people in spite of the fact most of them had never met anyone of a different race.

My grandfather reminded me of Superman. My father would describe him as fearless. He would approach a neighbor's house and walk right through 12 mean dogs.

My father and his siblings were very good at sports. The people in their little town ultimately fell in love with them, in spite of their differences. Over time, the townspeople grew very fond of our family and would even fight outsiders for disrespecting them. When equipment malfunctions or accidents occurred on the farm, families had no choice but to lean on their closest neighbors, who were generally five or ten miles away. When a tractor turned over, or a family was struggling to get the crop in before it washed away, people did not care what color you were. One of the most important lessons I received from my dad was if you treat people with respect and really care about them, they will do the same for you.

My father grew up learning you did not date outside your own race. He and my mother taught us that although it was all right to date a person of another race, we should marry someone black. My father also challenged us boys not to prefer lighter-skinned black women with long hair over darker-skinned black women with short hair. His concern was that we not let the values of the dominant culture cause us to devalue our own culture.

The Lessons that Shaped My Life

My mother and father were products of their generation. I understand that part of what my parents were seeking to do was to help us as children to maintain some level of pride in who we were. They also understood that the media did not portray people who looked like us in a positive light, so they invested extra time and energy to ensure that we did not view ourselves less than others based on the stereotypical images presented in the media. They would say, "You have to have pride in your race." Looking back, I can see how my parents really struggled with some of their own beliefs. The perspective they shared often seemed like more of a defensive move to protect us rather than one that supported their own core beliefs.

During my father's diversity trainings, he coined the term, "differential consequences". In short, he explained that minorities oftentimes had to prepare their children differently than dominant culture families because there was a greater risk they might be unfairly discriminated against based upon their race. While growing up, my mother was resolute in keeping her sons safe. She knew there were great risks involved in her black boys dating white girls. I will never forget my parents making me read the story of Emmett Till, the young black boy from Chicago who was killed while visiting his family in Money, Mississippi. Emmett was observed looking at a white woman while she was shopping; a bystander said Emmett whistled at the young woman. He was taken from his family's home by the woman's husband and brother, forced to carry a 75 pound fan, beaten with his clothes off, then tied to the fan with barbed wire, and thrown in the river. This took place in 1955. These kinds of stories put a great deal of fear in my mother. She wondered if something like this could happen to one of her four sons.

During the 1960s, the focus in the black community was on "black power", and "black is beautiful". The community was going through a revolution. You would not dare admit you were interested in dating or marrying a white female. It was clear if I was going to remain true to my community and my race, marrying someone that looked like me, which I ultimately did, was a major litmus test for loyalty to my culture.

We grew up with many of the same challenges people face in every family. We received some mixed messages. One message was that you had to love everybody and care for people, regardless of their race or socioeconomic status. The opposing message was that you had to socialize with people who were most like you. As a boy, I was told to date people who were attractive like us, smart like us, and black like us.

It is important for parents to recognize the powerful influence they have on their children. One of the most important roles parents have is developing basic values within their children. By the same token, we must prepare them to go beyond the narrow ways in which we see the world. Children must be able to see and engage the world through their own lenses. Furthermore, children should be taught that not every lesson their parents teach them will be correct. They must be able to go further than their parents' limitations.

De-Stigmatizing Prejudice

I would be a very wealthy man if I had a dollar for everyone who ever said, during a diversity seminar, that they were not "prejudiced." Our society has been successful at convincing people that being biased is not good. All of the marches, speeches, and sit-ins of the Civil Rights Movement have influenced us as a society that discrimination is wrong. I would even suggest this is the biggest diversity problem in our society, people declaring they are not prejudiced. If people believe that having prejudices is a bad thing, they often seek to avoid diversity training classes because they are often viewed as evidence that you are prejudiced. This posturing encourages people to conclude that progress on diversity insulates us from the need to attend diversity training classes. Therefore, it is critical we de-stigmatize bias so that people more readily own their personal shortcomings.

What is Bias?

Bias can be defined in many different ways. It is often used as a synonym for the word prejudice. In order to understand diversity, it is important to know the definition of bias. Webster's Dictionary defines bias as a preference or an inclination, especially one that inhibits partial judgment. Another way to define it is to be influenced in a particular, typically unfair or prejudiced direction. As a diversity trainer, I define bias as the internal negative feelings that are aimed at others who differ from you. Now that you know several ways to define the term bias, how do you differentiate a stereotype from prejudice or discrimination?

According to the Harvard Implicit Bias Project (HIBP), a stereotype is an exaggerated belief, image, or distorted truth about a person or group — a generalization that allows for little or no individual differences or social variation. Stereotypes are based on images in mass media, or reputations passed on by parents, peers and other members of society (HIBP). Prejudice is an opinion, prejudgment, or attitude about a group, or its individual members. Prejudices are often accompanied by ignorance, fear or hatred. Prejudices are formed by a complex psychological process that begins with attachment to a close circle of acquaintances or an "in-group" such as a family. Furthermore, prejudice is often aimed at "out-groups"(HIBP).

Discrimination is different than a stereotype or prejudice because it is a behavior that treats people unequally because of their group membership. Discriminatory behavior, ranging from slights to hate crimes, often begins with negative stereotypes and prejudices.

Define Four Types of Bias

According to the Harvard Implicit Bias Project, there are two types of bias that can exist within a stereotype; prejudice and discrimination. I offer two additional related biases that often influence Diversity Conversations. The four types of bias are:

- Implicit biases
- Explicit biases
- Surface-level biases
- Deep-level biases

Let us spend some time explaining the four types of bias. Implicit biases are biases that exist beneath the surface. They are the hidden and automatic preferences that favor certain human characteristics over others. The Harvard Implicit Bias Association group argues, "Scientific research has demonstrated that biases thought to be absent or extinguished remain as 'mental residue' in most of us. Studies show people can be consciously committed to egalitarianism, and deliberately work to behave without prejudice, yet still possess hidden negative prejudices or stereotypes" (HIBP).

On the other hand, explicit biases are preferences (positive or negative) that occur at the conscious level. People have a greater personal awareness of these types of biases. It is valuable for us to know our personal bias so we are better equipped to manage those biases that affect our relationships with others.

In workshops over the years, I have described people as being fairly comfortable with sharing their surface-level biases. I describe surface-level biases as those most people will admit or accept in others. Surface is specifically used to identify the shallow nature of the identified bias. It never fails that someone will suggest they are willing to openly share some of their biases and then say something like the following, "I really struggle with young men whose pants are hanging down to the ground." This type of bias only serves the purpose of re-enforcing negative stereotypes some people have about a certain group. Surface-level bias are often viewed as justifiable, and sharing them does very little to move the diversity conversation forward.

The last type of bias is the deep-level bias. This one is more difficult to admit to others. Deep-level biases are the immense biases we have against groups of people based on their race, gender, age, sexual orientation or physical appearance, just to name a few. Generally speaking, deep-level biases are viewed as unjustifiable. Therefore, it is difficult for people to comfortably admit to these biases. My experience has been that as people become more transparent about these deep-seeded beliefs, it can lead to a very rich conversation. However, there is a major risk in sharing deeper biases because they provide evidence others can use against you. Having facilitated numerous diversity conversations, I feel strongly that the opportunity for personal growth is worth the risk of backlash from sharing deep-level bias. Of course, where and how you approach sharing these biases remains a personal choice.

There is a significant benefit gained when people move from a posture of denial, fear, and complete ignorance of their biases to clarity, ownership, and accountability. As more people begin to admit their human frailty, there is less time and energy wasted on meaningless debates. It is critical that those of us who are given the opportunity to lead conversations about fairness and equity, recognize, own, and admit we too have deep-seated biases. In short, bias ownership is essential if we are to make substantial and sustainable progress in our efforts to build inclusive communities.

Diversity Conversations with Diverse Others

Diversity Conversations with diverse others can be the most challenging conversation of the three we will cover. In many ways, this entire book was written to help navigate diversity conversations with diverse others for meaningful outcomes.

Once in a while, on a sunny day, I will pull back the sunroof of my car, let down all the windows and change the radio station from peaceful music to one of the contentious, radio talk shows. One of the benefits of having XM Radio is there are as many liberal options as there are conservative ones. I let my mind go blank as the host fills the atmosphere with arguments and debates over any number of touchy subjects. Sometimes, I don't even listen to the words, yet I can still feel the emotional, negative energy of the conversations. We spend so much time debating differences. If however, we could somehow bottle the unconstructive energy that is wasted as people argue, we could probably balance the national budget, find a cure for cancer, and feed all the starving children in the world.

What are Diversity Conversations with Diverse Others?

As we reflect back on the dimensions of the diversity model, in Chapter Two, it is important to recognize that each of us is very diverse. Therefore, when we talk about having diversity conversations with diverse others, it is possible for people within the same race, for example, to have very different political or religious views. The conversations we want to focus on in this chapter are the exchanges that are most contentious and counterproductive. If we can do a better job of discussing diversity issues with people who are significantly different from us, we can certainly deal with conflicts that might arise when the differences are not so significant.

Who are the Diverse Others?

I have a good friend named Calvin. I met him in the mid 1990's as a result of teaching a diversity class at a local company. Calvin, like every employee at that company, was required to attend my diversity training course. He was a very talented young employee who seemed to have a bright future. Over time, we got to know one another personally and become friends, based on our common interest in sports. Several years passed and on a random visit to a community golf course, Calvin and I saw each other and got reconnected. We picked up where we had left off, with one significant change. This young, African-American man has become an outspoken conservative Republican. Over the years, I have met several conservative minorities, but it was rare for me to encounter someone who was so confrontational about their political views. My administrative assistant enjoys it when Calvin visits our office because his views align closely with hers. This particular example demonstrates that significant philosophical and political differences can exist between people of the same racial/ethnic group.

I want to encourage you to look at the Diversity Wheel in Chapter Two again. Review the various diversity categories; identify those differences that create the greatest challenge for you; for example, religious beliefs, sexual orientation, or race. Personally, I struggle with people who represent either of the political extremes, (strong Liberals or Conservatives). Therefore, I have to work very hard to manage my biases in order to take advantage of some of their valid points of view.

Brendan Nyhan, a researcher at Dartmouth College, conducted a study in 2005 to better understand people's ability to accept the truth based upon the strength of their beliefs. One insight gained was, "the more strongly the participant cared about the topic — a factor known as salience — the stronger the backfire" (backfire is the reaction some people have to facts in relation to their personal beliefs) (Nyhan, 2005). In other words, there are people, who feel so strongly about their beliefs, that when presented with true facts, they revert to their original beliefs more strongly. I must admit this study sent fear throughout my body. I began to question whether or not this book could have any impact on diversity conflicts. But then, I was reminded of the belief system I, and so many of you, grew up with. That is, "good is more powerful than evil and truth will ultimately prevail over a lie." My personal values give me confidence that we can work through our differences to find common ground.

How can we Better Manage Conflict with Diverse Others?

The following information may provide some helpful perspectives as we think about responding to conflict with diverse others. When listening to those who have dramatically different points of view, there are several responses to consider. You can be open, closed, learning, or challenging. Or, perhaps a combination of these responses is warranted.

Open

The word open can be defined as not closed, or unobstructed. When we describe open related to a diversity discussion, it means you are approaching the conversation with a willingness to learn; recognizing you could be right or wrong. To be open, a person has to have a degree of trust. On some subjects, I am open to different points of view; on others, I am not.

Closed

Closed can be defined as a barrier. In other words, when we are discussing an issue with someone and we are closed, it is very difficult for us to even listen to their point of view. People who are closed have already determined what you say is not going to make a difference. I know my faith is a subject on which I am fairly closed. I am, generally not interested in exploring what I might gain from adopting other religious beliefs. That does not mean I don't respect other people's right to believe differently. My personal faith is simply not open for debate. In short, it is a settled issue.

Learning

Learning can be defined as gaining new knowledge. One of the exciting opportunities available every day is to learn something you did not know the day before. Many of the most successful corporations we've worked with have defined themselves as "learning organizations". Unfortunately, the beginning of failure is when a person, or an organization, decides they no longer need to learn. Some may even describe this posture as arrogant. Some notable organizations, at the height of their success, decided they no longer needed to learn from their customers. Other organizations have gone so far as to proclaim they create their customer's desires. Clearly, there have been several successful organizations over the years that have generated market demand through an innovation; however, there are significantly more examples of organizations that no longer exist as a result of ignoring the interests and needs of their customers.

Challenging

The word challenging means to push back or take exception. Some people were raised never to challenge authority. Others were brought up to challenge everything they hear. Regardless of your upbringing, it is important you stand up for what you believe. If you feel strongly about a truth, it is imperative you stand behind what you believe. By the same token, it is counterproductive to challenge with no regard for the truth. For those who commit themselves to argue and fight no matter what, they will bear the cost of their ignorance. What is more frightening is our society bears the cost of delayed solutions.

We should recognize the value of engaging in productive and respectful conversations with people who see the world differently.

Consequently, it is more helpful to be open versus closed. Openness allows people to gain new insights that may, or may not affect their personal belief systems. If people are closed, then it is important they clearly understand the consequences of their behavior. There are situations where people may be learning and challenging others simultaneously. Both of these responses have value if they are used in the right situations. This really boils down to knowing when to be the student and when to be the teacher. Both roles have the potential to create personal growth.

Now that you have a better understanding of how to approach diversity conversations with diverse others, the next chapter provides an example of a major challenge that makes all three diversity conversations difficult.

References: Harvard Implicit Bias Project.
https://implicit.harvard.edu/implicit/
Keohane, J. (July 11, 2010). "How facts backfire: Researchers discover a surprising threat to democracy: Our Brains". The Boston Globe
Sagan, C & Durian, A. (1992), Shadows of Forgotten Ancestors. Random House Publishing Company: New York. Webster's Dictionary

Diversity Story Chapter 5

"Same People - Different Sides"

What do Bill Maher and Rush Limbaugh have in common? Let's see -- talk show hosts, obnoxious, smart, smart-alecks or maybe sexist. Many of the media prognosticators have been criticized for sexist comments they made about women. Bill Maher has referred to Congresswoman Michelle Bachman, and Governor Sarah Palin in shockingly sexist and disrespectful ways. Rush Limbaugh's comments about Georgetown law school student Sandra Fluke, were broadcast around the country as a new low in media insensitivity. This prompted President Obama to personally call Ms. Fluke, as a sign of support.

Most people would say Maher and Limbaugh were dramatic, with a bias toward being sensational talk show entertainers. The success of these two media moguls would suggest that many people, including those reading this book, support them, their communication style, and the philosophies for which they stand. I have listened to each of them on more than one occasion. I even, at times, find them both entertaining, but, increasingly, I've become concerned that their blended approach of political satire, legitimate news, and entertainment is done at a great cost to cultural and political unity. Each of them attempts to increase the level of paranoia within their most loyal followers. Their perspective seems to be that there is a villainous opponent who seeks to control and destroy all that is of value to us. The 'us' is never fully defined, but somehow refers to hard-working, good-natured, legitimate Americans. There are people who work to drive a wedge of division between those who have different points of view. I've created a name for them and that name is "Professional Diversity Polarizers (PDPs)".

Chapter

5

Professional Diversity Polarizers

"The people who make a living through Dividing Others"

As mentioned in the introduction, I have been attempting to write this book for over 16 years. The diversity challenges we are facing in this country and around the world have given me the focus and passion to finally accomplish this life-long goal. I have been frustrated, and, at times, angered by the declining interest many people have in identifying common ground between those with opposing points of view. It is even more disconcerting to see professionals use polarization as a tool to generate and maintain interest in their specific platform. This chapter will describe a specific category of people I refer to as "Professional Diversity Polarizers" (PDPs). It will also touch on ways we can reduce the conflict they create between ordinary people.

If there are antagonists in this book, they are PDPs. They are sometimes referred to as loudmouths, talk show hosts, or sensational reporters who distort information for their personal gain. They are individuals who attract a lot of public attention and are compensated, typically, very well, due to their ability to draw and maintain loyal followers. These disreputable individuals are called PDPs. The word professional is used because they get paid for the job they do, whether in money, or influence. They are also called professional because of their skillful abilities in persuasively communicating their particular points of view. Diversity hot topics are attractive to PDPs because these issues often cause strong emotional reactions from large groups of people. When people become emotionally charged, it is hard for them to walk away from a discussion, or turn to another station. It seems to me whenever there is a slow news day, talk show hosts will raise issues of race, sexual orientation or religion. It seems like a shameless strategy used to ensure that PDPs maintain and grow their audience. PDPs sometimes argue about issues in which they personally have no real interest or concern.

The word Polarizer is used to describe PDPs because their approach causes people to adopt extreme points of view that otherwise may not have been espoused. This chapter seeks to answer the following four questions:

1. What do PDPs do?
2. Why do people follow them?
3. Why do they matter?
4. How should we respond?

What do PDPs do?

PDPs are professional communicators who talk to us over radio and satellite airwaves, through television, and cable, over the internet, and in newspapers, magazines, and blogs and other media/communication vehicles. PDPs are also extremely effective in the delivery of their messages. Their style and information enable them to garner large audiences through the use of strong, and often controversial, points of view. They seem unafraid to speak their mind and present candid issues the average person might avoid in public discourse. PDPs generally present one side of an argument and dismiss other views. They suggest their message is balanced, honest, and true. This subjective deceitfulness may be the most dangerous aspect of a PDP. They present themselves as objective citizens in search of solutions that are in the best interest of all people. They also describe themselves as being willing to take risks based on the compassion and concern they have for their listeners. PDPs have many different personalities. They may be, funny, serious, or passionate and they too have their own dominant and non-dominant diversity traits. Ultimately, their main objective is to stir-up audiences in order to secure and maintain a loyal following over time.

Why do people follow them?

PDPs are often smart and interesting in order to maintain the interest of their audiences. These individuals, often times, do incredible research, selectively pulling out pages of data to support their position. Ted Koppel on the television program Rock Center on Sept. 13, 2012, identified the partisan machines used by both Democratic and Republican parties to do nothing but collect gaffs, mistakes and misstatements made by their political opponents. They are often referred to as "watch organizations", but they actually are major research arms for both liberal and conservative people and institutions. Beyond being entertaining, people follow PDPs because they speak to issues of importance to their audiences. People enjoy listening and watching PDPs who boldly and unapologetically, articulate their point of view.

Diversity debates are oftentimes viewed in much the same ways as sporting events. People generally keep score of how their team is doing in these on-going cultural debates. When people have to listen to diverse perspectives, they often get an internal sense their team, or perspective is losing ground. When they hear people articulate their point of view, they feel like maybe their side is making a comeback, or even winning the debate. Finally, the average person just needs something, or someone to believe in personally. I do not believe every aspect of a PDPs message is negative. I do however, feel strongly that people are used as pawns in the PDPs overall strategy. Their ultimate objective seems to be self-promotion and growing their followers.

Why do they matter?

It's important we get a sense of why PDPs matter. First, they matter because PDPs bring a degree of honest perspective to our national discourse on diversity. Without PDPs in our society, we may be forever trapped in politically correct and semi-honest discussions about diversity. By definition, PDPs break the political correctness mold. Secondly, PDPs present weaknesses, or risks that exist, as society focuses on building an inclusive environment.

PDPs also give voice to important perspectives shared by those in their listening audiences.

The downside of PDPs is they typically create wedges of separation between people, making it far more difficult for people to find common ground with each other. Prior to the last three U.S. Presidents being sworn into office, I felt passionately that their number one strategy as the Commander-in-Chief was to work with the best people and ideas on both sides of the political landscape. Even through negative campaign advertisements, you can see there are intelligent people supporting both the Democrat and Republican parties. With each new President, I have been tempted to buy a full-page newspaper advertisement saying, "Please bring our country together."

However, President Barack Obama's election made it painfully evident how difficult unity is to accomplish. President Obama ran his presidential campaign on a platform of inclusion. Many declared his election as evidence that we had moved into a post-racial period in our country. Once elected, I thought he made an effort to work with leadership across the aisle. Unfortunately, it was not well received. I was a bit surprised that Democrats were just as challenging for this new President. It appeared the Democrats were saying, "You are simply one guy and you need to align yourself with us in order to be successful." The Republicans made it clear their number one job was to ensure he was a one-term president (McConnell, 2009). What I learned was it was somewhat naive to believe that people can easily build bridges with political opponents. Herein lays the great strength of PDPs. They are not seeking to bring people together. Rather, PDPs are attempting to deliberately divide. Unfortunately, that division has a cost we all must bear.

The major cost related to PDPs is the reduction in our societal capacity to negotiate and develop mutually beneficial solutions. Our Declaration of Independence stated: We the People -- and clearly recognizes that in order to co-exist, people are going to have to compromise to accommodate diverse interests, diverse needs, and diverse aspirations. One of the major costs of PDPs is they gain life from division and increased negative emotion. PDPs have as their main objective to advocate single-sided solutions. They drive up paranoia in people and promote the notion that success in our union is a zero-sum game. In other words, the mentality is the pie is only so big, if others get more then we get less. This strategy becomes overwhelmingly effective during difficult economic times. Furthermore, the average person does not have enough time to engage in his or her own research, so they are left defenseless as prey in the talons of these predatory media moguls.

How should we respond?

At the end of the day, we are free people living in a free society. None of us can begrudge others for the freedom they have to live how they want to live. According to our Bill of Rights, Americans have free speech so they can do what they want to and say what they want to. So, people are ultimately responsible to be as informed as possible on issues that matter most.

I generally go through a full range of emotions from joy and laughter to anger and frustration as I listen to PDPs. While PDPs are performing their magic on us, we in turn, become more engaged in increased conflict among our fellow citizens. The strategies utilized by PDPs come with a cost. So, we must work to better understand and effectively manage diversity conflicts by better understanding the five basic conflict styles, or the preferred way of behaving in various situations. Blake and Mouton Managerial Styles research has been adapted to incorporate contrasting conflict styles as impacted by diversity. It is important people are knowledgeable about their personal conflict style. It is also critical for people to determine how to respond to conflicts they encounter, especially disagreements about diversity.

5 Types of Conflict

1. **Avoidance** is characterized by behaviors that either ignore or refuse to engage in conflict. While avoidance is presented by some theorists as a negative style that shows low concern for individual interests, there are sometimes strategic reasons to avoid conflict (Blake & Mouton). For example, when the relationship is short-term, or if the issue is not important, or when the situation has a potential to escalate into violence, avoidance may be the prudent choice. Examples of avoidance behaviors include:

- Saying an issue is not important enough to spend time on.

- Stating there is not enough time to do a specific topic justice.

2.   **Competition** or a win-lose mentality is a style that maximizes an individual's ability to reach his goal or get problems solved at the expense of the other party's goals or feelings (Blake & Mouton). While always choosing competition has negative repercussions for relationships, businesses and cultures, it can occasionally be the right style to choose if the other party is firmly fixed in a competitive style or there are genuinely scarce resources. While competitive tactics are not necessarily dysfunctional, competition can easily slide into destructive scenarios. Understanding this tactic, and the strategies of others who use competitive styles, can assist you in defusing the negative consequences of competition in order to work toward mutual gains. Examples of competitive tactics include:

- Concealing one's own interests and goals
- Elevating one's own arguments
- Denying responsibility
- Pretending to be or actually being hostile

3.   **Accommodation** involves giving into another individual's wishes in order to smooth the choppy waves of a conflict. Accommodation sacrifices an individual's goals for the sake of the other person. When one party in a conflict genuinely does not care about the outcome of the conflict, accommodation may be the right choice for that situation. However, if accommodation is the

only style a person utilizes, he should practice using other conflict styles. Examples of accommodators phrases are:

- "Whatever you want is fine with me."
- "The group's decision is fine with me."

4.   **Compromise** involves a focus on give and take. The classic compromise in negotiating is to "split the difference" between two positions. While there is no victor from compromise, each party moves away from simply focusing on their goal. Examples of compromise are:

- "I will give you this if you give me that."
- "We will split the difference."
- "We will agree to disagree."

5.   **Collaboration** occurs when parties cooperatively work together until a mutually agreed solution is found. For any conflict, this is the optimal solution for both parties.

According to Scott Landon in Collaboration and Community, examples where collaboration works best include:

- Cultures that encourage participation, rooted in a practical concern, for the topic as a whole.
- Realistic and commonly accepted visions that take into account the strengths and weaknesses of each individual.
- Effective building-block organizations that blend the self-interest of its members with the broader interest of the community and translate that dual interest into effective action (Landon, 1995).

Responding Effectively to Diversity Conflict

There are many ways to respond to conflict situations. Some styles require great courage, while other styles necessitate great consideration for the other party. Some styles are cooperative and others are competitive, while other styles are quite passive. There are five different ways people can respond to heated diversity conversations: 1) Walk Away, 2) Cave In, 3) Stand Your Ground, 4) Compromise and 5) Collaborate.

Walk Away

In addressing diversity conflicts, clearly one of the strategies available for you is to simply walk away. For some people that may sound weak. But, the first thing to determine is whether this is your natural conflict style. After determining what your natural style is, know there are four ways of walking away. Selecting this strategy can lead to the right choice, wrong choice, weak choice, or strong choice.

When Walking Away is the Right Choice

Growing up, I did not receive a lot of encouragement to walk away from conflict. I was educated to never walk away. As an adult, walking away is sometimes the absolute right choice, especially around the topic of diversity, which creates strong emotional reactions.

Having the opportunity to observe different conflicts, there were some conflicts where people were protesting a certain issue like abortion or the right to life issues. If you are passionate about these topics, then you probably would not walk away from these debates. However, if you are not versed on this topic, you may want to walk away. Another example is when Cincinnati, Ohio went through its civil unrest in 2001. There were significant and emotionally charged conflicts that erupted during regular City Council meetings. On a couple of occasions, I saw people argue so aggressively you got the sense it was going to escalate into something beyond just an exchange of words. When you are engaged in any conflict and it begins to feel unsafe, sometimes walking away is the right and best choice. Additionally, if you feel you would say something you might regret later, walking away is probably the appropriate choice. However, by knowing your natural style, you can prepare yourself to utilize other styles that may be more effective in a given situation.

When is Walking Away the Wrong Choice?

Sometimes walking away is simply the wrong choice. Diversity conflict in and of itself is not a negative thing. There are biases, belief systems, and points of view people may express that are immoral or simply wrong. In some of these situations, walking away or ignoring bigoted comments or behaviors may be the wrong choice. There may be times when you are engaged in conversations with friends and they tell an offensive ethnic or gender related joke. It may be appropriate to address their insensitive comments.

When is Walking Away the Weak Choice?

Sometimes walking away is simply the weaker choice. If progress in our society is to be made, at times, we need to display a greater degree of courage. There may be situations where we may be around influential people. They may be saying things that are contrary to what you know is true about a certain group of people. In this example, walking away is a weak choice. As I continue to grow and mature, it is no longer acceptable for me to ignore gross generalizations made by people within my racial group about others who are different. For example, if someone in my race says, "You know how those folks are," or "They're all like that," I generally address the issue head on. Although there is always room for each of us to grow, this narrow-minded thinking has become increasingly unacceptable to me. There was a time when I would just ignore these types of comments. But the older I get, I view walking away as a weak and personally unacceptable choice.

When is Walking Away the Strong Choice?

One of the places people experience a great deal of conflict is in relationships, most notably, marriages or long-term relationships. You really learn a lot about yourself in the midst of these kinds of interactions. Over the course of my marriage, there have been a couple of times where my wife has challenged me in ways no man ever would. Moreover, there have been occasions where we have become really upset based on the other person's points of view. Some of those conflicts have been related to diversity issues, but most have been about how to best raise our children. I tend to be more traditional and old school. But, my wife tends to be more lenient and certainly more patient when it comes to how the children complete their homework and chores. I can say unequivocally that our diverse approach has led to better overall decisions despite our occasional disagreements and conflict.

There have been times when I know I have angered my wife. On one particular occasion early in our marriage, she was under a lot of stress and we were arguing about a minor issue that became major. I said something that made her so angry she took her arm and swept all of my neatly arranged watches off the nightstand. Anyone who knows me is aware that I have a large collection of different watches. The scene felt as though it was moving in slow motion as I watched my beautiful watches fly through the air and onto the floor. Her frustration level had gotten so high as a result of my stubbornness, she lunged toward me with her arm drawn back as if to hit me. I grabbed both of her forearms but then quickly made the decision, I needed to just walk away. Walking away in this situation was not only the right choice, but it took strength to do so in the heat of the moment. The way I was raised, if someone confronts you with an attack, you literally fight back. In this particular case, walking away meant not only leaving the room, but leaving the house for a period of time. I got in my car and drove around the neighborhood giving us time to calm down. My wife has never been a violent person, not before and not since that event. But sometimes difficult conflicts can push us toward more aggressive responses, especially if you have a close personal relationship.

Walking away gave me an opportunity to think about what I had said that enraged my wife. Once we had the opportunity to calm down, I recognized the insensitive nature of my comments and apologized. After 20 plus years of a successful marriage, we laugh about this story today.

Cave In

The cave in conflict style seeks to give in as opposed to demonstrating the courage to fight for your point of view. I am not a big fan of caving in, but on a daily basis, it is a choice followed by countless people all across the country. The best way to describe the caving in conflict style is with this example. You happen to be from a family that is very conservative. You were raised with Ronald Reagan's picture over the fireplace in your living room. Therefore, you have a lot of personal admiration for President Reagan and regard him as one of the greatest leaders of the 20th century. During a conversation with a friend from your child's school (this person happens to be a very vocal liberal) you failed to stand up for your beliefs. This friend had been to your home on a couple occasions mainly because your children enjoy playing together. On one particular day, your friend begins to aggressively criticize President Reagan even though she has heard you mention your respect for him and his legacy. In this scenario, if you begin to verbally agree with her, when inside your mind and heart vehemently disagree, you would be described as caving in. Caving in is when you take a position contrary to what you really believe. It is very difficult to make diversity progress if people simply abandon their belief and cave in to others. So, why do people cave in? I do not have an easy answer, but I think there are some people who are easily persuaded by another person's point of view. There are others who just do not feel strongly enough about anything; while, there are others who identify with the path of least resistance. Whatever the driving force, while I do not see a lot of value in caving in, respecting a person's ideas without verbally agreeing or disagreeing may be the best solution.

One might ask, "What is the harm in caving in?" I believe there are several problems with this conflict style. First and foremost, I do not believe it is honest. In order for us to make diversity progress, people have to share honest points of view. Secondly, caving in can lower an individual's self-respect and the respect received from others. It is important for people not to confuse caving in with compromising, as these are two completely different conflict styles. Caving in is being passive, while compromise takes more work on the part of people on both sides of an issue.

Caving in not only harm the individual who caves, but it hurts the person they are debating. Unfortunately, one trait I have observed among those engaged in diversity conflicts is this self-righteous attitude people may have about their point of view. Therefore, allowing individuals to remain unchallenged in their narrow view is not a healthy choice.

Caving in is different than walking away. Walking away is a conscious decision that continuing a conflict may not be worth the energy. Whereas, caving in sends a message that the other person's point of view is valid or correct when in fact it may be invalid.

Stand Your Ground

This style seeks to compete with other points of view. Standing your ground means you feel strongly about your point of view and are unwilling to compromise your perspective in order to resolve a conflict. I can relate to the standing your ground approach in diversity conflicts. Unfortunately, this style at times can make it very difficult for people to find solutions to their diversity conflicts.

Compromise

Compromise is often described as finding a win-win solution to achieve common ground. Compromise happens when people are willing to mutually identify agreed upon solutions to their conflicts.

Collaboration

Collaboration is working together to achieve a goal. It is a process through which two or more people work together to realize a shared objective. When you compromise, it is a settlement of differences by mutual concession. In other words, this is an agreement reached by adjusting the conflict, opposing claims, or principles by reciprocal and modified demands.

Collaboration has clearly lost its value in our national political discourse between the major parties. However, it can never lose its value to ordinary people. We must recognize the power of compromise and not allow collaboration to be re-defined by those seeking to limit choices and control the point of view of others. Wise and fair compromise is evident all across the greatest success stories in America's rich history.

The next chapter is powerful. It ties all the principles you have learned to assist you in working to resolve diversity conflicts in future conversations so you can gain multiple perspectives to find common ground.

References:

Blake, R.; Mouton, J. (1964). The Managerial Grid: The Key to Leadership Excellence. Houston: Gulf Publishing Company.
Landon, S. (1995) Community and Collaboration: Pew Partnership for Civic Change; Washington, D.C.
http://www.youtube.com/watch?v=W-A09a_gHJc

Diversity Story Chapter 6

"The Older I Get, The Better I See"

In my family, playing sports was a big deal. Although my dad talked a lot about school and the value of education, you could see that special light in his eyes when he talked about sports. So for my siblings and me, sports played a very big role in our lives.

The two longest walks I ever took were related to sports. The first was the day I was cut from my high school basketball team. Basketball was my father's favorite sport. When I was growing up, he used to tell us about his days playing college basketball. He shared that he played with Oscar and Bailey Robertson. You could feel the enthusiasm and love he had for the game. I inherited the same passion for the game. So I played basketball my first three years of high school. When I came back as a senior, we had a new basketball coach and he decided to cut me from the team in favor of some younger players. I'll never forget that day.

It was shocking to me that I was no longer defined as an athlete. I wasn't sure how I would break the news to my father. I took that long walk home. My father was very encouraging and shared with me that no one could ever determine when your athletic career had ended. He said if you want to get better, you have to spend a lot more time practicing. He told me that Oscar Robertson slept with a basketball, so that's what I did. I ended up attending Anderson College in Indiana. This was a college both my parents attended. When I got there, I tried out for the basketball team. With great excitement, I made the team. After two years, I transferred to Wright State University (WSU) where my father was the Assistant Dean in the School of Professional Psychology. My first year there, I couldn't try out for the team because I had played at Anderson. Consequently, my father and I got to spend a lot of time together. He and I would fantasize about me trying out for the basketball team at Wright State University. They had a national reputation and making the team would be a big challenge and great honor. I remember my mother dismissing my father and me as two dreamers lost in a basketball "twilight zone". I never fathomed that my first year at WSU would be my father's last year of life. The summer after my first year, he died of a massive heart attack. He was a very significant influence in my life. There was one overarching thought that sustained me after his death. The dream we shared of me trying out and for the Wright State basketball team. It was that thought that brought me back to college in the fall. So I tried out for the team, worked hard, and felt as though I was competitive with the other members of the team. But I wasn't sure I would make the team. The last day of tryouts arrived. The coaches announced they would post the roster in the main gym later that afternoon. I went back to my campus apartment and several hours later I took the second longest walk in my athletic career. I arrived at the gym and ran into the assistant coach. He was speaking and I was listening, but I couldn't follow anything he was saying. The final statement I heard him make was "You need to pick up your sports equipment downstairs". It hit me like a bolt of lightning. I had made the Wright State Raiders basketball team. I went to the equipment room, got my sweatshirt and shoes, and danced all the way back to my room. The excitement continued as our team went on to win the NCAA Division Two National championship. We played our final game on ESPN. I felt as though my father was in heaven slapping "high fives" with some of heaven's coaches about his kid.

After we won the national championship, I was invited back to my high school to speak to players on the basketball team. I was very careful not to display any bitter feelings about being cut as a senior. But on the inside, probably for the next two decades, I felt as though I had been treated unfairly. It's interesting how we see things more clearly as we age. Today, I have a better understanding of how a new coach might focus more on younger players than a senior. This chapter presents a concept I refer to as "diversity critical thinking". My objective is to help people understand the legitimate points of view that exist on opposing sides of any particular issue.

Chapter

6

Becoming A Diversity Critical Thinker

7 Step RESPECT Process

Most people know the difference between right and wrong, but each person has the freedom to establish and maintain his or her own personal belief systems. Some people believe in life after death, while others believe in reincarnation, and yet others believe when we die, we are simply dead. But, what if your beliefs on death are wrong? Or, what if someone who views death in a way completely different from yours is right?

Another idea to consider: What if a person has a better understanding of truth than you? Would you want to know that truth? I do not think anyone would intentionally choose to live in a fantasy world, believing their views are right when in fact they are wrong. Unfortunately, many people choose fear over facts and untruthful ideas over accuracy. Our belief systems do not come with a "fact referee," or an expert who knows all the right answers to life's difficult questions. Since there is no omnipotent person to provide us with immediate and irrefutable evidence about the truth of our perspectives, we are left to make our own calls and determine for ourselves whether our beliefs are correct. Regrettably, we are not always objective, and at times, we make judgments in favor of our (sometimes) misguided belief systems. Therefore, it is imperative each of us grasp how important it is to become a critical thinker about diversity matters.

Chapter Six will begin with basic knowledge about how our brains work and the influence mental models have on our views and ultimately, our capacity to improve being competent about diversity. This chapter will also provide a practical definition of Diversity Critical Thinking (DCT), why DCT is important, and the seven steps you can take to apply this skill when faced with diversity conflicts or impasses. Finally, the DCT tool will be explained with examples so you can apply it to your diversity conversations in order to find common ground.

Diversity Critical Thinking

Diversity Critical Thinking (DCT) is an ability to understand and articulate many of the complexities involved in effectively discussing and resolving diversity-related issues. DCT is the skill to accurately identify various (and often opposing) perspectives that exist in specific diversity issues. DCT is also a process, or tool, that can help us collect valuable data regarding opposing viewpoints in an effort to discover the objective truth. There are several key behaviors that demonstrate an individual's effectiveness at DCT. They are self-awareness, being inquisitive, and delaying certainty. We must understand the underlying characteristics of DCT in order to resolve diversity conflicts and find common ground. Let's explore each behavior.

DCT Behaviors

Self-Awareness

People who are effective at DCT generally know what they believe and why. They are also aware of their principles and how those principles influence their behaviors. They are conscious of their personal hot buttons regarding diversity. For example, if a person recognizes they have very little patience with people who are narrow-minded, then they would have a higher degree of self-awareness than someone who doesn't recognize their shortcomings. Although not everyone is born effective at DCT, anyone can learn to apply these skills in daily conversations. Consequently, people who are most effective at DCT, have an elevated degree of self-awareness, which often translates into being a more effective communicator.

Being Inquisitive

In order to be effective at DCT, people need to have a willingness to search for the truth that exists beyond their common understanding. To be effective at DCT, you must possess a willingness to challenge personal paradigms, or patterns of thinking. This is not natural, as most people seek predictability and comfort. To successfully apply this DCT skill, you must recognize that there are valuable insights that exist among those with whom you disagree. Ultimately, the goal is to determine what is right, as opposed to who is right. Furthermore, the capacity to genuinely accept the validity of opposing points of view expands your knowledge and leadership skills.

Willingness to Delay Certainty

DCT means you accept the uneasiness that accompanies being undecided about an issue or group of people. If people cannot delay the gratification of certainty, they will not exhibit effective DCT. The process of examining difficult, emotionally-charged, diversity issues takes time, so it is important to take the necessary time to collect additional information about diverse perspectives. Those who apply this behavior will undoubtedly gain benefits even if their original perspective does not change.

Becoming a diverse critical thinker may be the single most important concept in this entire book. No matter where you stand on an issue, it is critical to utilize tools that can help you avoid the limitations of ethnocentrism and narrow-minded thinking. It is useful for people to have the ability to technically and dispassionately map out the core issues that comprise diversity conflicts, reframing long-held mental models.

Mental Models Defined

Mental models are the images in our head we have about people or specific situations (Johnson-Laird, 2005). Figure 2.1 demonstrates the information/input into our brains through our five senses.

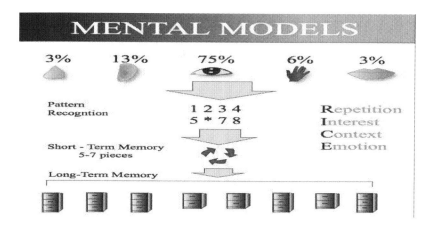

Figure 6.1 Mental Models

Over time, we begin to recognize patterns, and those blueprints are stored in our short-term memory and eventually into our long-term memory. This memory creates mental models.

Sensory Input

Seventy-five percent of the information we obtain comes into our brains through our eyes, thirteen percent through our hearing, six percent through our touch, and three percent each through smell and taste (Hauger, 1997). This new information is often received from interactions with our families, friends, neighborhood and the media. Once input comes in, the brain begins to recognize patterns.

Pattern Recognition   a b c d

e f * h

If I were to ask you to describe the pattern above, most people would describe it as the alphabet. If I were to ask you what did not fit in the letter sequence, you would easily recognize that the asterisk does not fit. However, if I asked you how you knew that answer, you might respond by saying you grew up knowing that information. In short, you know what fits and what does not in much the same way we collect data from our families, our neighborhood, and the media. These patterns originate in your short-term memory.

Short-Term Memory

Most people can hold between four-five pieces of information in their short-term memory. It's difficult for us to hold a lot of information in this part of the brain. For example, when I am talking to somebody on the phone, I may ask them for their phone number, which they will provide. I remember the 7 or 10 digits at that moment, but we continue to talk a few more minutes before hanging up. Unfortunately, I forget the number so I have to call and ask for his number again. Have you ever experienced a time when you failed to pick up an item while at the grocery store for someone else? Regrettably, when you return home, the person was disappointed because you did not remember the item. It is the limitations of our short-term memory that places us in this predicament.

Long-Term Memory

There are four things that move information from our short-term memory to our long-term memory. They are described by the acronym **R.I.C.E.**

R is for *Repetition*, or the things we hear over and over and tend to remember over time.

I stands for *Interest*. Information we are interested in, we will tend to remember over time. I love Stevie Wonder's music. So, it is not difficult for me to remember Stevie's music because it is something I enjoy. On the other hand, if you were to ask me to describe the different kinds of plants that decorate the side of the road between my house and my office, I would not have a clue because plants are not a topic I take pleasure in studying.

C is for *Context*. Information can be remembered over time based upon the specific circumstance in which an event occurs. For example, if I ask you to remember something that transpired during your high school prom, the context may help you recall an important memory.

E stands for *Emotional Events*. If information is tied to a significant emotional event, then you are more likely to remember it over time. People are often asked to recall where they were when John F. Kennedy was assassinated. Those who are old enough can remember with great detail where they were based on the significance of the event. Many Americans remember where they were on September 11, 2001. This was the day terrorists flew planes into the World Trade Center in New York City. That event will live on in the minds of millions of people for the rest of their lives.

In short, mental models become the lens through which we see the world and the pictures we have about people who are different. The only problem with these models is if the information or inputs we receive are inaccurate, then the mental models, or stereotypes we have, are also incorrect. Another major problem that exists with mental models is once these images have been established; it may take the force of dynamite to blow them apart.

Mental Models In Action

In order to better understand how mental models influence your behavior, I am going to ask you to reflect on the following description. You are driving in an urban area in a major city. You look around and there is trash blowing down the street. Many of the businesses have boards nailed up against their windows. You are not feeling particularly safe, so you take a quick glance, to make sure your doors are locked. You pull up to a stoplight and all of a sudden, an older gentleman with a grey and black beard stumbles up to your car and knocks on your window. What color is he?

Now, assume you have driven out of that area and are on the interstate traveling away from downtown. While driving, you see lots of trees and smaller buildings. After a 15-minute drive, you get off the exit and notice a large, beautiful shopping mall. Your favorite store, Nordstrom, is facing you. You quickly park your car because you notice a sign that says, 'Spring Shoe Sale!' As you get out of the car, you forget to lock your doors. Inside Nordstrom, a wonderful, very helpful woman asks if you would like to try on some shoes that have caught your eyes. What color is she? You do not stay at Nordstrom very long. You walk down the hallways of the mall and see Victoria's Secret. How would you describe the people who work there? Are they attractive or unattractive?

By now, you may be confused because you may say that no one in particular comes to mind. But for those of us who are familiar with these stores or similar locations, specific characteristics of people came to mind as each environment was described. Those images are also mental models.

Our Brain Matters

Our brain works to protect the things we believe. When an argument ensues, it is not natural to immediately seek to better understand the other person's point of view. Our mind operates in much the same way as red blood cells respond to an injury. When the body is cut or injured, red blood cells rush to the injured location in order to heal the body as quickly as possible. When diversity conflicts arise, our brain often focuses on giving us as much information as possible to retain and strengthen our current beliefs.

Figure 6.2: Universal Diversity Impact

Personal Mental Model Identification

Looking at the diversity wheel in figure 6.2; as we discussed in Chapter 1, there are three dimensions of diversity: Personal, Social, and Organizational Dimensions. Select one particular category from the wheel. For this example, I will highlight the personal dimension of personality. When we think about personality, most of us determine whether a person is an introvert or an extrovert. Think about which term best describes you. Introverts are individuals who generally get their energy from internal reflections. Extroverts, on the other hand, usually get energized from interactions with others. Now, take a minute to think about which term best describes you, but write down as many descriptors as you can about the other personality trait.

As an extrovert, here are my descriptors about introverts. Introverts are: smart people, not very talkative, boring, and not very popular. Now select a category from the wheel that tends to be more emotionally charged or polarizing. Some examples might be religious beliefs, race, or sexual orientation. During workshops, I ask people to write down everything they have read, heard, felt, or believed about a certain characteristic. It is important that people are honest and select those things that immediately come to mind. I also ask participants to describe the words they wrote as descriptors of the different characteristics. The majority of participants typically put together a negative list of descriptors. As you look at the information you recorded, would you describe it as positive or negative? I would place a bet that there are more negative descriptors than positive traits. Furthermore, like workshop participants and their descriptions, the majority of information that is most readily available about diverse people tends to skew negative. When diversity conflicts arise, recognize the impact of your personal beliefs.

The average person recognizes fairly quickly which side of an argument lines up close to their own belief system. Unfortunately, very few people recognize and accept that there are legitimate opposing points of view. So as we seek to diagram an argument, it is probably best to approach this process like lawyers preparing a defense strategy for a big trial by carefully researching both sides of the argument.

I will never forget watching the Perry Mason television show when I was a child. For those old enough to remember, what made Perry Mason such an effective lawyer was his ability to anticipate the strategy used by opposing counsel. We have learned over the years, you cannot make progress by simply spending more time studying your personal point of view. You also need to work hard to understand the position of those disagreeing with your viewpoint. The best law firms literally engage in mock trials among their own lawyers as rehearsal for real trials.

I would like you to identify a recent disagreement you may have had around diversity. Take a piece of paper, divide it in half and put your perspective on the left side and write the opposing perspective on the right side. As you think about the other person's point of view, try to identify some valid arguments.

The Value of Diversity Critical Thinking

As people increase their ability to think critically about diversity, they improve their overall ability to grow individually. Diversity Critical Thinking (DCT) is about expanding your knowledge beyond the limitations of your current comprehension. The mere act of exploring the validity of opposing points of view creates personal growth. This process engages you to continuously learn. It also reduces destructive conflicts and enables you to exist more harmoniously with diverse people. DCT also provides people with an objective tool to help resolve diversity conflicts that exist between individuals. Before you get started on the diversity critical thinking process, there are several key areas you must assess. It is important you evaluate your own desire and readiness to begin this process. You should also determine whether or not you have a sincere desire to work on personal diversity conflicts. You must also be aware of the difficulty of this process. Furthermore, you must have a sense of how strong your beliefs are on specific diversity topics. The higher your emotional attachment to your point of view, the more difficult it will be for you to utilize this process without significant assistance from advocates of the opposing point of view.

Diversity Blind Spots

Each individual should have some sense of his or her own diversity blind spots. These hidden areas represent our inability to hear certain information due to pre-existing belief systems that create barriers. Often when individuals have very strong belief systems, it is difficult for them to accept information that contradicts those attitudes. I was not surprised by insights gained by University of Michigan researchers regarding an average person's inability to change their mind based upon facts. In a series of studies in 2005 and 2006, researchers found that, "when misinformed people, particularly political partisans, were exposed to true facts in news stories, they rarely changed their minds. In fact, they often became even more strongly set in their beliefs. Facts, they found, were not solving misinformation. Like an underpowered antibiotic, facts could actually make misinformation even stronger" (Kaohane, 2010). The study found that, "Rather than facts driving beliefs, our beliefs can dictate the facts we chose to accept" (Kaohane, 2010). In other words, people have mental blockers that make it very difficult for them to hear accurate and truthful information.

7 Step DCT *RESPECT* Process

The Diversity Critical Thinking *RESPECT Process* is a tool that will help resolve diversity conflicts. The *RESPECT Process* below will enable you to solve diversity issues in a methodical way. This process has been successfully utilized by thousands of individuals as a part of my training seminars on diversity. Individuals from a variety of backgrounds have mentioned this methodology as one of their most important takeaways from our training. Simply stated, this process enables you to identify both sides of a diversity issue in an effort to find common ground.

> **R:** Recognize Diversity Conflicts and Write up a Statement
>
> **E:** Evaluate the Strength of your Beliefs
>
> **S:** Set a Specific Goal for your Diversity Conversations
>
> **P:** Prepare a DCT Diagram: 2 Major Points of View
>
> **E:** Establish 3-5 Supporting Points of View
>
> **C:** Common Ground Statement
>
> **T:** Take Action to Improve your Diversity Conversations

R: Recognize the specific diversity conflict or issue that you are seeking to address. Diversity is a broad subject so the nuances are very important. Therefore, it is critical to take time to clearly identify a diversity conflict statement. (For example: There is a debate going on in our country regarding education. Some people believe public schools need the resources and support to improve. Others believe that families need vouchers to give them the freedom to choose what school their children will attend.)

E: Evaluate the Strength of your Beliefs

One area that will impact an individual's ability to effectively utilize DCT is the strength of a person's attachment to his or her own viewpoints and personal beliefs. The greater the attachment, the more difficult it is to apply DCT to a particular conflict or issue; the lower the attachment, the easier it is to utilize DCT. Belief strength can range from a low to a high value and can be rated using the following scale: (1 low-level attachment to your point of view to 5 high-level attachment to your point of view).

This self-rating scale is intended to assist you in determining how important it may be to identify advocates to aid you in being more objective as you begin developing your DCT Diagram. If you know you have a very strong emotional attachment to your belief, then you will need to spend significantly more time consuming information that supports the point of view you oppose.

S: Set a Specific Goal for Your Diversity Conversations

It has been said that if you do not know where you are going, any road will get you there. I would say that if you do not establish a goal for utilizing this tool, you will never know when you have achieved your objective. I feel strongly it should be your ultimate goal to better understand diverse perspectives to reduce your ignorance regarding difficult issues. It would be helpful if more people worked harder to establish common ground with people who have diverse view points. So, decide from the outset what you want to achieve through DCT. Three options are provided below:

- A better understanding of different points of view
- Convincing others of the validity of your point of view
- Finding common ground between diverse points of view

P: Prepare a DCT Diagram

The DCT Diagram is the physical tool that will be utilized to begin mapping out your diversity conflict or issue. Initially, it is recommended that you physically go through the process of diagramming the specific case you have identified.

Divide a piece of paper in half and leave room for titles at the top of each side of the paper. (Over time you may choose to simply go through this process in your head).

Identify 2 Major and Opposing Points of View

One of the most important steps is identifying the two major and opposing points of view. Generally, if you are in an active discussion or debate it may be difficult to write down the major points of view. It is strongly recommended that you take some time to make sure each of you has clearly stated your point of view. If you are going through this process alone, you can fill in responses to the following steps:

1. Write the points of view in descriptive and non-judgmental language.
2. Identify which point of view is most consistent with your personal beliefs.

3. Make sure you accurately identify the opposing point of view and not simply write down your negative impressions of perspectives that differ from yours.

E: Establish 3-5 Supporting Points of View

Once two major points of views have been identified, it is necessary to provide additional supporting points. It can be very difficult for anyone to identify the legitimate points of view of those who oppose their viewpoints. I would encourage you, if time permits, to do the following:

a. *Identify* and ask for input from advocates with different points of view (i.e. someone who is aligned with the opposing perspective).

b. *Research* those sources viewed as valid by those with opposing points of view.

C: Common Ground Statement Development

You should review the key you acquired throughout this process and create a statement of common ground. By developing this statement, you will be prepared to achieve any goal you establish as it relates to conflicts and issues about diversity. You will also be prepared to engage in far more productive discussions with those who see the world differently.

T: Take Action to Improve Diversity Conversations

Finally, in order to improve the results we gain when engaged in difficult diversity conversations, we must practice effective communication techniques. There are thousands of articles and books that can help you improve your communication skills. One of the most important skills is effective listening skills. Therefore, if you are in a difficult conversation with someone regarding diversity, actively listen to them and paraphrase their point of view. After we have taken the time to improve our thinking relative to diversity issues, we must communicate in ways that will improve the likelihood of experiencing a more respectful conversation.

Figure 7.1: **The 7 Step DCT *RESPECT* Process**

R: Recognize Diversity Conflicts and Write up a Statement

_____

_____

E: Evaluate the Strength of Your Beliefs

      1   2   3   4   5

  Low   High

S: Set Specific Goals for your Diversity Conversation

_____

_____

P: Prepare a DCT Diagram; 2 Major Points of View

    1. _____

    2. _____

E: Establish 3-4 Additional Supporting Points of View

    1. _____   2. _____

    3. _____   4. _____

C: Common Ground Statement

_____

T: Take Action to Improve your Diversity Conversations

_____

The Paul Ryan Case Study

Now that you have placed this "Amazing New Tool" (smile) in your tool chest, let's see how useful it is in a real life situation. Personally, I find politics fascinating in part due to the critical role communication plays in our decision-making process. Politics is also interesting theatre because it is far more socially acceptable to publicize your beliefs and stereotypes about opponents. While the rest of society is running around hiding their prejudices, politicians and pundits are saying anything television advertisers and cable stations will allow.

In March 2012, Senator Paul Ryan, a young, rising star within the Republican Party, shared that his Catholic faith had influenced many of his priorities in the Congressional House Budget he authored. Although the comment about his faith was not a major point in his presentation, it generated a surprising and significant backlash among a chorus of Catholic bishops, theologians, priests, social justice leaders, and nearly 90 Georgetown University faculty and administrators. The group was so upset, they signed a document criticizing his statement that his faith was a guiding force in developing the budget. There was one person in particular, Jesuit Father Thomas J. Reese, a Senior Fellow at the Woodstock Theological Center at Georgetown University, who took direct aim at the Senator by saying, "I am afraid Chairman Ryan's budget reflects the values of his favorite philosopher, Ayn Rand, rather than the gospel of Jesus Christ. Survival of the fittest may be okay for Social Darwinists but not for followers of the gospel of compassion and love."

Father Reese signed a letter from The Catholic Bishops sent to Senator Ryan that made many points critical of the Senator's use of Catholic teachings to justify his budgetary actions and priorities. "We would be remiss in our duty to you and our students if we did not challenge your continuing misuse of Catholic teaching to defend a budget plan that decimates food programs for struggling families, radically weakens protections for the elderly and sick, and gives more tax breaks to the wealthiest few." (Reese, 2012)

Reflecting on Diversity Blind Spot

My administrative assistant is one of the reasons I have been able to complete this book. She and I agree on many things, but politics is not one of them. She spent many hours listening to me start and stop this book, making a few grimacing faces of disapproval. However, there has been an interesting learning that has taken place throughout this process for each of us. As we were working on this particular section of the book, we stumbled upon a wonderful teaching moment. We had an opportunity to see firsthand how difficult it can be to even hear the facts when we have a strong belief about the perspective held by others. I was describing the importance of objectively stating both major points of view when we are diagramming a diversity conflict. I stated, "It's important for you to reflect on where you stand as it relates to the Paul Ryan and Father Thomas Reese disagreement. She immediately commented, "You didn't share Senator Ryan's position." I was shocked by her response because I had just recited several points the Senator made. She had typed them, yet never heard them. I asked her to go back and re-read what I said and what she typed. It was not until we slowed down the entire process and she went back to carefully read what I had stated as Senator Ryan's perspective that she realized I had in fact identified several major points given by the Senator.

I identified these points from Senator Ryan's point of view:

I.   Our government spends too much money.

II.   If our leaders do not balance the budget, we are literally going to be passing debt on to our children and grandchildren.

III.   It's not good for able-bodied people to continually be in a cycle of receiving support from the government. So for him, his efforts to reduce the national debt are very important.

IV.   The government needs to get out of the way of the private sector (reduce unnecessary regulations) and develop policies that support job creators.

The key learning we took away was that it could take a significant amount of energy and focus to avoid our diversity blind spots. They exist without our knowledge and can make it very difficult to find common ground. This example is typical of diversity conflicts that arise on a regular basis. It is surprisingly difficult for most people to step back from important issues to objectively identify diverse perspectives that may exist. It is very important, at times, to literally diagram the diversity conflicts objectively.

One might conclude that people spend very little time thinking critically about diversity. There are few people who take time to diagram diversity arguments in order to ensure they are approaching the discussion from a balanced and fair standpoint. When someone demonstrates the ability to be a critical thinker, we generally view them as reasonable and capable of resolving difficult diversity conflicts. So, the next time you watch a pundit debating a topic, I encourage you to use the DCT Process to sort through the information they present. While using this model, it not only will make you a stronger critical thinker, you will be able to more effectively discuss and consider other viewpoints objectively and rationally.

References: Hauger, J.D. (1997) Business Consultant. Global Lead LLC: Cincinnati, Ohio.

Johnson-Laird, P.N., (2005). Mental Models, Deductive Reasoning, and the Brain.

Kaohane, J. (July 2010). "How Facts Backfire" Boston Globe.

Reese, T. (2012) An Open Letter to Senator Paul Ryan.

Diversity Story Chapter 7

"Principle of the Junk Yard Dog"

On one particular day, I was conducting a training seminar in southern Indiana. There were 14 participants and none of them looked excited to be in my class. The class started a little slow and the group was fairly quiet. My expectation for success was diminishing with each hour that passed. Most of the participants had stated in their introductions they weren't very open to diversity and were wondering why they were forced to be there. That is generally a sign the two-day training seminar could become more like a marathon than a sprint.

A tough, seemingly uninterested, audience generally presents a challenge to me as a facilitator. I typically see my goal as moving a group of people from resistant, to valuing the principles of diversity. This particular group was 100% male and 80% farmers. Whenever I'm training a group like this, my farming roots tend to surface. I tend to talk more like a Hoosier. With all the effort I was giving, there was very little evidence this particular group was making any progress. Then out of nowhere a reluctant participant raised his hand, and I could see a bit of excitement in his eyes. He exclaimed loudly that finally he understood what diversity was all about. He shouted, "I got it! What you're trying to say is that it's easier to recognize that junk yard dog when he's got you by the ankle." He said it so fast I missed it the first time. So I asked him to slow down and say it again. He repeated his statement and this big 'aha' came over the entire class. He was saying it's easier to recognize problems when they have a direct impact on you. We may not even be aware of serious issues that others encounter.

I share this story hoping it will inspire you to a greater openness to the perspectives of people who are different from yourself. The opportunity for each of us is to be open to learning more about the challenges others who may be different from us, face.

Chapter

7

Putting It All Together

Diversity Conversations must be Intentional vs.
Accidental

I bet you can hear the band playing and see the parade coming down the street. Congratulations! You have arrived at Chapter Seven, the final chapter of this book. Now it is time to put all your new knowledge to use. This entire book has been written in an effort to better prepare you to be more thoughtful about many of the most challenging diversity issues we face today. This particular chapter is divided into two major sections:

Section One will focus on presenting six difficult diversity issues or "Hot Topics." The goal is for you to read the issue and then utilize the 7-step DCT *RESPECT* process to prepare a balanced view of the legitimate points of view that exist on both sides of the argument. The ultimate goal is to work, where possible, to identify common ground.

Section Two is a collection of tips and insights from our professionals. I have invited some of our most effective senior diversity consultants to share some of their experiences relative to diversity conflicts. These individual contributors have been evaluated by our clients as highly effective at leading diversity conversations across a broad cross-section of people. We are very appreciative of the talents, gifts, and abilities they have cultivated over the years. They will share their personal story; provide some expert insights, as well as practical tips that have enabled them to effectively resolve diversity conflicts over the years.

SECTION ONE: Diversity Hot Topics

Each of the following topics has received significant publicity over recent years. I have highlighted certain aspects of the issue for the purpose of this chapter. Read each of the hot topics and then select one or more of them to diagram using the Diversity Critical Thinking Process.

Once you select your diversity hot topics, your task is to diagram two major opposing issues that exist as well as three or four of the most significant sub-points that exist on each side of this issue. It is important to take the issue you selected through each step in the DCT process in order to improve your ability to better understand each perspective and to identify common ground that may exist between people who see this issue from diverse points of view. The seven-step process is outlined in figure 7.1, at the end of the chapter, to serve as a guide to support you through this exercise.

Diversity Hot Topic #1
Valuing Differences vs. Ignoring Differences

Individuals who are members of traditional diversity groups feel strongly that most organizations need to establish special efforts focused on encouraging organizations and their people to value differences. There are also a large number of individuals who feel that many of the problems we face regarding diversity are a result of focusing too much on our differences. They believe that the best way to deal with improving relationships across different groups of people is to ignore their differences. This hot topic will be used as a sample for you to follow.

7 Step DCT *RESPECT* Process (sample)

Step #1   **R:** **Recognize** the diversity conflict and write a statement. Each hot topic represents a conflict statement. Take time to review the hot topic statements you've selected.

Step #2   **E:** **Evaluate** the strength of your belief. As I reflect on Hot Topic #1, my belief is fairly strong that individuals and organizations need to establish specific strategies to ensure they value human differences. I would score my belief strength a 4.5 on a 5-point scale in terms of how strongly I am invested in my Point of View (POV).

Step #3   **S:** **Set** a specific goal for your diversity conversation. Step three provides an opportunity to identify what my specific goal would be in a conversation with someone who would have a different perspective than my own. My goal, at this point, would be to convince others of the value of my POV. I would want to make sure that I am respectful of their POV and could demonstrate that I recognize some of the legitimate reasons people may disagree with my perspective.

Step #4   **P:** **Prepare** a diversity critical thinking diagram, including the two major points of view. It is useful, at this stage, to go back and review the conflict statement and based on that statement;

write down the two major and opposing points of view. You may want to get a separate clean sheet of paper. First write down each opposing POV. It may be helpful to begin by writing down the POV that most closely aligns with your personal beliefs.

POV #1   I believe individuals and organizations need to be intentional and deliberate in their efforts to value human differences. It will not happen on its own.

POV #2   There are others who strongly believe it is best to ignore differences in order to treat people fairly.

Once you have written the two broad POV statements, you can summarize them in two-to-five words for the diagram.

Summarized POV #1: Conscious Effort to Value Differences
Summarized POV #2: Ignoring Differences Ensures Fairness

Therefore my DCT chart would look like the one below:

POV #1: Conscious Effort to Value Differences	POV #2: Ignoring Differences Ensures Fairness

Once you have the DCT diagram set up, you will be prepared to move to step #5.

Step #5   E: **Establish** 3-4 additional supporting POV for each major POV. The additional points should be written directly onto the DCT diagram.

POV #1 Conscious Efforts to Value Differences	POV #2 Ignoring Differences Ensures Fairness
1. Valuing differences does not happen naturally or easily. You have to work to ensure you are being fair.	1. If people focus too heavily on differences that may create greater division.
2. Our biases exist privately in our minds and are generally acted upon discretely.	2. If you focus more on being fair and less on human differences, you will automatically help all people.
3. Without taking deliberate actions, we generally do what is most comfortable.	3. When people focus on differences, bias and discrimination are created.

Step #6   C: **Common** Ground Statement Development

This step requires you to establish a new statement, which seeks to establish common ground. My common ground statement for hot topic #1 is the following: "It is important that people make a conscious effort to treat people fairly while not simply focusing on differences for differences sake."

Step #7   T: **Take** action to improve your diversity conversations (i.e. actively listen and paraphrase). This step invites you to identify several specific actions you can take to improve the quality of your diversity conversations related to hot topics. Step Seven also provides an opportunity to reflect on the goals identified in step three and determine if they still apply and what actions can be taken to change or accomplish them. I have listed some specific actions below:

- Meet with someone who holds the opposite POV.
- I still support my original goal and will seek to achieve it through respectful conversations with those who hold a different POV.
- Do some additional research on the opposing POV to determine if there are key points I am overlooking that could cause me to change my personal perspective.

Diversity Hot Topic #2
Immigration: Border Protection/Illegal Immigration vs. Humane Immigration Reform

Illegal immigration to the United States has been a long-running controversial issue in our country. America is a nation of immigrants and yet this issue is a major flash point for both large and small communities. One aspect of this issue relates to individuals who illegally reside in this country. There are some people who think the majority of our focus should be placed on securing our borders and deporting those who are in America illegally. There is another perspective that encourages more compassion for non-dangerous, undocumented workers.

Diversity Hot Topic #3
Freedom of Speech vs. Culturally Sensitive Language

Our nation was built on the notion of free people being able to speak freely. By the same token, there are people who want others to keep track of their ever-evolving descriptions and identifications of their group. An example might be someone who has lost the use of their legs desires to be referred to as "differently-abled" vs. "disabled". So there is a conflict that exists between the values and desires of different groups. It is important that people have the ability to clearly understand the different viewpoints. The First Amendment of the United States Constitution protects freedom of speech in the United States. However, this freedom is not absolute; the Supreme Court of the United States has recognized several categories of speech that are excluded from freedom of speech, and it has also recognized that governments may enact reasonable time, place, or manner restrictions on speech.

Diversity Hot Topic #4
The Definition of Marriage: Protecting Traditional Definitions vs. Expanding the Definition to the LGBT Community

One of the most controversial issues in the United States revolves around the definition of marriage. There are some who feel strongly the term marriage has significant social and economic benefits that should be extended to all committed couples, irrespective of their sexual orientation. There are others who are equally passionate that the term marriage should be reserved to legally define the relationship between one man and one woman who have committed themselves to each other for life. The following information provides some perspective on this issue currently. Approximately 75% of the states have passed laws which define marriage as limited to a union between one man and one woman; 33 state legislatures have passed statutes to that effect, and four states have, by popular vote, passed the Defense of Marriage Act (DOMA) as a constitutional amendment. Thirteen states do not currently have laws on their books, which limit marriage to a union between one man and one woman (CLGS, 2012). There are people on both sides of the argument who feel very strongly about this subject.

Diversity Hot Topic #5
Economic Recovery: Democrat vs. Republican Strategies

At the end of the second term for President George W. Bush, the national and global economies were experiencing a major free-fall. Most Americans were introduced to a term they were not familiar with at the time; *economic stimulus*. President Bush introduced a bill to Congress seeking $800 Billion to be pumped into the banking industry in order to buffer our nation from entering a Depression.

Newly elected President Barak Obama continued along this path, bringing forth a second economic stimulus in an effort to help the economy recover from the recession our nation was experiencing. For the entirety of President Obama's first term in office, there has been a significant national debate regarding the best strategies to bring about economic recovery. In general, the Republican Party has been focused on lowering taxes, and reducing government spending. The Democrats have been focused on lowering taxes on those who have incomes less than $250,000, raising taxes on the wealthiest in our nation, and closing tax loopholes on the wealthy.

Diversity Hot Topic #6:

Gun Violence: NRA Perspective vs. Gun Control Advocates

There has been a long-standing debate in this country over gun rights. The Second Amendment to the United States Constitution is the part of the United States Bill of Rights that protects the right of the people to keep and bear arms. It was adopted on December 15, 1791, along with the rest of the Bill of Rights.

A major issue in our country revolves around gun violence. There has been an ongoing debate regarding where responsibility lies. There are some people who feel strongly that gun violence has a direct relationship to the legal access people have to guns. The gun control advocates believe it is important to restrict the overall number and types of guns available. On the other side are gun supporters and enthusiasts. Some might argue the most powerful special interest group in our country is the National Rifle Association. This group has a whole myriad of goals and objectives. One of their most significant objectives is to protect the freedom of all law-abiding citizens to have unrestricted access to guns. They feel strongly that more effort needs to be put into taking action against law-breakers and not against guns.

References: http://www.clgs.org/marriage/state-definitions

Figure 7.1: **The 7 Step DCT *RESPECT* Process**

R: Recognize Diversity Conflicts and Write a Statement

_____

_____

_____

E: Evaluate the Strength of Your Beliefs

       1   2   3   4   5

   Low   High

S: Set Specific Goals for your Diversity Conversation

_____

_____

P: Prepare a DCT Diagram; 2 Major Points of View

   1. _____

   2. _____

E: Establish 3-4 Additional Supporting Points of View

   1. _____   2. _____

   3. _____   4. _____

C: Common Ground Statement Development

_____

T: Take Action to Improve your Diversity Conversations

_____

SECTION 2:   Hearing from the Professionals

Karen Townsend, Ph. D.

Someone once asked me, "When did you know you were black?" Initially, I had to think about it? I wanted to respond by saying, "I have known I was black all my life." But then I considered the question more critically. When did I know I was black?

I grew up in an all-black family. I lived in an all-black neighborhood. I attended kindergarten with seventeen other black students and was taught by a black teacher. While both my doctor and dentist were white, the fact that their skin color was different from mine really didn't impact me at the time.

When I started first grade, I went to a school that now as an adult, I realize was predominately white. My two best friends were Kathleen (who was black) and Julie (who was white). We LOVED each other! I can remember our mothers making us matching outfits—corduroy miniskirts with matching vests. Mine was pink, Kathleen's was blue, and Julie's was yellow. Like our matching outfits, our skin color was different, but it didn't really impact me at the time. The next year, my family moved and I went to a new school. It was on that first day at the new school I finally realized I was black. Or maybe more accurately, I realized what my blackness meant to many people around me.

As I was introduced to my new classmates, I distinctly remember a girl named Angel. (In retrospect, her name was most inappropriate!) While the other children in the class welcomed me and said "Hello," Angel looked me straight in my eyes and added her own one word greeting—"Nigger!"

To this day, when I think back on that experience, I am wounded once again. I was hurt and confused. Why would she say such a thing to me? Was it because I was black? What did it mean to be black? What did it mean to be different? For the first time in my life, being black impacted me.

Perhaps it was that early experience with Angel that planted the seed in me to become an advocate for those who are under-represented and often disenfranchised. While my response to Angel as a seven-year-old was just as inappropriate as her comment (I slapped her face as hard as I could), today I work as a certified diversity consultant. Although that early experience with diversity was quite negative, I am now committed to helping individuals and organizations recognize the benefits of diversity. While we acknowledge the rapidly changing demographics of the 21st century, the most successful organizations will be those who not only recognize diversity, but also possess the awareness, knowledge, and skills to leverage the diversity around them.

As a seven-year-old, I didn't possess the diversity critical thinking skills to assess my situation and respond appropriately. Angel—who may have had only limited exposure to a person who looked like me—obviously lacked those skills as well. She spoke based on limited information about me, who I was, and the group I represented. My physical assault of her was based on heightened emotions and hurt feelings. We would have both been better served if someone would had simply asked the difficult question, "Why did you use that word?"

How many times in our adult lives have we witnessed, overheard, or perhaps even participated in conversations where inappropriate language was used to describe a person or group? How might that conversation have been changed if someone had simply asked, "Why did you use that word?"

My diversity journey began over four decades ago as a hurt and confused seven-year-old girl: one lone black girl in a predominately white second grade classroom. Today, as a nearly fifty-year-old woman with a Ph.D., I still find myself in situations where I must make a choice; wanting to slap someone's face or asking a question. I have found the better choice is to ask the question. An amazing thing happens when we have the courage to ask; most people are willing to talk. And if we are successful in getting people to talk—to have what might sometimes be a difficult conversation—this often serves as a first step in promoting understanding among and between diverse groups of people. Thank you Angel, for launching my diversity career!

Sandy Wheatley

Recently, I was facilitating a Diversity and Inclusion class for a group of hourly employees at a manufacturing company. At the end of the session, a young African-American man came up to me and said these words, "I know I can say this to you 'cause you proved yourself cool today. Thanks! For an old white chick you really get this conversation." I believe this just might be the nicest compliment I have received in my 15+ years of facilitating the conversation of diversity inside corporate America.

As I drove the four hours home from that session, I reflected on when it was I began to "get this." Those reflections eventually led me to asking "when did I realize I DIDN'T get this?" That journey started about 17 years ago when I had the privilege of attending a diversity awareness seminar for a group of educators in my school district. Until that time, I knew I had an intuitive sense about bringing value to people, but until someone really challenged me on how I connected the dots to get to the decisions I made, I didn't know what I didn't know.

As I began to navigate discussions about diversity with a variety of folks, I realized that "diversity" was right up there with the big three your mama told you to never discuss in public...sex, religion and politics! When I did find myself embroiled in a diversity conversation, it was because someone, somewhere, had said or done something seemingly crazy. All of a sudden everyone had an opinion, was free to share it, and were lining up on one side of the topic or the other.

I believe that is what makes conversations about major diversity issues so difficult. We rarely had them with one another until Rodney King was beaten up, Henry Lewis Gates was being arrested on his own front porch for breaking and entering, or Hillary Clinton weeped at the podium. Now the 24/7 media coverage and conversation becomes more about who's right or who's wrong and less about listening.

When people find out my professional life involves facilitating the conversations of diversity for a variety of businesses across the country, I am often asked, "What's been your toughest diversity conversation?" I think they expect me to say one that involved race or sexual orientation. Actually one of my toughest was trying to convince a group of Board of Education members to provide diversity awareness for all our employees.

For twelve years, I served as a member of the Board of Education for the school district in the community in which I live. We were a school district in transition going from being 98% white to having a 10% (and growing) minority population. We were beginning to have people question our motives and decisions as racially/ethnically biased. As a board we talked about the need to lead the district through some diversity awareness conversations, but no one on the Board of Education wanted to call it diversity. They wanted to clean it up, call it something else, so it wouldn't, "scare people or give them reason to think we were caving in to 'those people'". Because they had their own bias or mental models about the word "diversity," they were paralyzed to move forward and provide an opportunity for teaching and learning to occur. Thus, NOTHING was done!

I believe our school district as well as our community had been well served if early on we would have embraced an opportunity to engage in DCT. I believe this is one of the most powerful tools a person can possess in order to be a change agent in the communities where they live, work and play.

I use DCT all the time in a training setting, particularly when a "hot topic" gets thrown out and people get excited about their point of view. First I teach the concept, then we role play the principles using a typical workplace statement. However, the real learning comes when after four hours in class they are arguing about, i.e. "If you want to live in this country you have to speak the language and we shouldn't cater to all these people by giving them language options." I make them choose one of two sides of the issue and do the diversity critical thinking techniques. It is amazing how many times you will hear someone say, "I never thought about it that way."

So am I an "old white chick" who gets this diversity conversation… some days yes and some days I think I haven't a clue. But what I do know is I have committed, until I draw my last breath, to asking the question, "What might I be missing that is a part of your reality is not a part of mine?" I am convinced if more of us developed this habit we would resolve more issues and find more civility in our everyday lives.

Barry Myers

I grew up in a racially diverse neighborhood and my early mental models about racial diversity as a white male were that everyone was familiar and comfortable with it. In college, however, I remember an afternoon sitting in front of the library with a classmate who commuted from a distant suburb. "Barry" he said, "can you believe how many black people are here on the campus?" I looked around carefully and counted about one of ten students were black. I was confused by his question. "What do you mean?" I said. "Well," he answered, "there are so many blacks here." That, for me, was an "aha" moment when I first realized each of us has varying degrees of exposure to racial diversity and often it is based on where we live and where we grow up. It challenged my mental models and it is an important signpost I can point to on my journey of diversity.

Engaging people in meaningful conversations about our backgrounds can be challenging if it evokes concerns from individuals they might be perceived as biased or prejudiced. I think there is a belief in our society, often taught by our parents or teachers, that it is wrong or unacceptable to have bias or prejudices. But don't take my word for it. Try an experiment with a friend or colleague and say, "I have noticed you have bias against (fill in the blank here)." Give it a try. I guess your friend or colleague will cross their arms and say "No I don't. I don't have any bias against (fill in the blank)." I make that prediction because I have caught myself crossing my arms and saying "No I don't". Yes, I am defensive and insecure about my biases and prejudices. So, getting past political correctness and establishing a safe and supportive environment to discuss our biases is the first step on a journey to self-awareness.

One of the most challenging moments I encountered as a facilitator was leading a diversity class comprised of Japanese managers. I vividly recall when a mid-level Japanese engineer began citing injury statistics on a specific assembly line and attributing the cause to an engineering design flaw. We often think, myself included, the Japanese are demure and averse to confrontation. I formed this opinion after living in Japan for five years. The following case would challenge not only many westerners' mental models but even my own about the Japanese. I observed an offended engineer, the one that supervised the assembly line in question, cross his arms, stand up with a crimson red face and engage a raging debate with his counterpart while the rest of the class watched transfixed as reality-show confrontation unfolded with surprising vitriol. So, even as a professional, I still catch myself challenging my own mental models.

Cultivating self-awareness of my mental models provides fertile ground to think critically about how I manage diversity in my daily life and accurately survey the landscape of my journey; a journey that is much like life itself. So there is always room for me to learn and grow. Learning to be mindful and dwell in the present moment in my interactions with people – especially those most different from myself – has actually become an activity I have come to savor. And because I make a conscious effort to be agile with critical thinking about diversity while on my journey, I find myself crossing my arms much less than I used to when I first started this journey.

Deborah Kendrick

The first time I felt discrimination in a personal way, I was 16.
I had just come back from applying for one of the summer jobs offered by the local board of education, where my solid self-confidence had been diminished to a quavering question mark and replaced by a heap of self-doubt.

The job duties included typing and answering phones. I'd been a whiz typist since the age of eight and my telephone manner was borderline legendary. Given my popularity in our large suburban high school, my role on student council and in the National Honor Society, the part I'd played in winning medals for our forensics team and gymnastics extravaganza, I fully expected to be hired on the spot.

But the response when my dad and I arrived couldn't have been clearer: Blind girls need not apply. Stung with disappointment, I stood on our sunlit porch with my dad, an epiphany forming like the proverbial light bulb in my head: This, I told him, must be what it feels like to be black.

I had always been the only kid in school who was blind, who had any disability really, and I'd never given it much thought. Sure, sometimes I needed an alternate way of doing things – sculpture instead of drawing in art class, putting my hands on the skeleton to learn the bones' names in physiology – but it was no different from being short or tall, alto or soprano.
Or so I thought.

As my world grew larger, I became increasingly aware that this thing about me, this characteristic of needing to see things with alternative methods, this characteristic I could not change about myself, would always run the risk of putting me in the "other" category as I encountered those whose sight was too narrow to really see me.

I went to college, graduate school, got married, had three beautiful children. Each new adventure – from starting a co-op nursery school in our church basement to launching a career in freelance writing – involved "selling" a few people along the way on the reality of my being more "like" than "unlike" my fellow travelers.

Other mothers trusted me with their children. Editors favored me for assignments. But I never knew when a perfectly lovely day might be interrupted by the waitress in a restaurant who would baffle my four-year-old by telling her to "help Mommy" or by a fellow journalist at a press conference who would mistake me for an observer rather than a colleague. Still, my life, both personally and professionally, was filled with blessings, and educating others to see me as just one more human being was a part of my life script. Then one day life itself, the life of my child, hung in the balance.

My seemingly perfect marriage of 22 years was suddenly derailed by tragedy. It happens sometimes. Divorce was not something either of us had anticipated, but here it was. Two years later, a worse crisis came in the form of a custody battle.

The court-appointed social worker initially saw only my blindness. "How can you know what your child is wearing?" she asked. "How can you know what she is doing?"

I explained, but knew I wasn't getting through.

Then, I called an editor of a magazine for which I'd written a column on parenting as a blind person for nearly fifteen years. "Send me everything I've written that might help this social worker understand that a blind parent can be a good parent," I asked her in desperation. She did.

After receiving that packet of articles, the social worker called me into her office. She happened to be black.

"I owe you an apology," she said. "I was asking you questions that I realize now came from my ignorance of a culture different from my own. As a black woman, I know all too well what it is like to be the target of such ignorance."

In the end, I was awarded sole custody of my daughter.

My work as a writer and speaker and educator is largely centered on helping people see that we are all more alike than we are different. Another blind person might not be a good mother, but I was. Another black woman might not have been a good social worker, but she was.

By having the "conversation," we each saw the other first as just a fellow human being. That is what having diversity conversations can do for all of us.

Cathy Scrivner

The following four diversity encounters, stand out in my mind, and has shaped who I am.

The first experience was when I entered kindergarten as the only black child in the class. This was the first time I truly recognized I was different. I didn't understand why, but it was clear my teacher didn't like me. It was her tone, her look, her body language. She always hugged the other children, and never so much as touched my hand. She always selected me last, even though my hand was the first to be raised. I kept thinking I had done something wrong, so I tried even harder to make her like me and picked her flowers, brought her candy, and made her cards. Because of her continued ill treatment towards me, classmates alienated me as well. I was lonely and I was hurt. One day I finally spoke up and said, "God can't love you because you are so mean to me!"

The second experience was in the fourth grade when I had a best friend named Phyllis. She was unpopular, awkward, nerdish-- with glasses, very quiet, and always wore dated un-cool clothing. Of course I didn't care about any of this, because I was just happy to have someone who wanted to be my friend. Since I talked about Phyllis so much, my mom invited her to spend the night, and we had a blast. In turn, her mom invited me over also. When her father met me and discovered I was black, he called Phyllis in the other room to speak to her. I overheard him tell her, "She can't come over again, 'cause she's a nigger. We can't have niggers in our house." Phyllis never told me what her father said, but our relationship was never the same after that.

Thirdly, in 1978, I was the only black cheerleader on my high school squad. Our team was scheduled to play in a town known for their racism, and although I was concerned about going, I didn't want to let my squad down. As I was cheering on the field, someone threw a brick, hit me in the head, and briefly knocked me out. The squad dragged me under the bleachers, and eventually escorted me to the bus to wait, while they finished cheering the final quarter of the game.

Finally, I graduated from Indiana University (IU), with 39,000 students and 1,200 African-Americans. As a freshman, I sought my counselor's advice on classes to take the second semester. Her recommendation was to leave IU to make room for "other" more deserving students. She suggested I make it easy on myself and leave before the upcoming semester because I would probably be like most of the other African-Americans and not graduate.

These four events impacted my life significantly, and for the longest time I wished I was white, so I could be accepted and valued. It took years for me to develop confidence, and actually like the person God created me to be. Today, thinking back on these experiences is painful, and the memory of my hurt is as vivid as the day they happened. From these experiences and others, I knew I wanted to be part of the solution for understanding differences. So many times throughout my life, I had been the one and only, and spoke on behalf of what seemed to be the entire black population, when really, I just wanted people to see and understand me. Facilitating diversity conversations has been a gift to me as I have been able to help many by promoting understanding. Equally as important, I've grown to better understand my own biases, self-esteem issues and self-talk. Yes, as a 51 year old professional, I am still healing.

I find diversity conversations difficult for three reasons. One, many of us are arrogant about our past experiences and knowledge, which leads to an unwillingness to seek more information about differences. Two, there is a fear of losing our "rightness" if we make room for other peoples' perspectives. Finally, we don't take enough time to reflect on our own histories to recognize we have some biases and understand how they impact our relationships with others.

I witnessed and personally experienced this very thing when I was challenged with a diversity conversation I facilitated about sexual orientation. It was 2002, and for the first and only time in my diversity career, I had a participant in the class come out of the closet. It was silent for what seemed like an eternity, but then, the conversation quickly turned to everyone wanting to weigh in on their perspective. It was extremely difficult to navigate because of the huge gap between perspectives, and the strong passion and emotion, which exuded from each side. I've found the more opinionated and passionate we are, the more difficult it is to listen to other's experiences, or ask questions. The "aha" moment for me was when I could not only see the struggle the class participants had with the conversation and their biases, but I recognized I had my own biases from messages I had received from my parents, community and faith. I could see that I personally needed to do more work on this particular subject and get more information to manage the files in my own mind. Thank goodness I've done the work, and I am still working!

There is a tremendous value of diversity critical thinking when you have two opposing viewpoints, such as I did when I facilitated the above sexual orientation conversation. Diversity critical thinking is the ability to walk around a diverse topic, and look at it from all sides. To recognize there is texture and many layers to a diversity point of view, and to be able to identify what is legitimate in a view that is completely different from yours. When we acknowledge what's legitimate, we move the conversation along in a productive way. We may never fully agree with the opposing view, but we may be able to validate some parts of their perspective, and use that as a foundation for true learning and listening. It's less "us against them," or "he says his stuff, and I say mine" bantering, with the goal of understanding. It's been a privilege to participate in the education of diversity and the impact of differences. In addition, every diversity conversation has allowed me to progress in my own journey of diversity, and I'm grateful for that.

Robin C. Gerald

Prior to starting my consulting practice I worked for a company that was sued for racial discrimination and, in order to comply with a court decree, rolled out mandatory diversity training for 5,000+ employees. That two-day learning experience changed my life for the better personally and professionally. It was the beginning of my diversity journey, yet if given a choice, I know for sure I would not have attended. You see, as a woman of color I had a narrow view of diversity and felt I was already an expert on the topic simply because of those dimensions. In addition, I had been "raised right" and knew before I entered kindergarten that I should treat others the way I wanted to be treated, never judge a book by its cover, always be nice and respectful. I was well educated, had good intentions when interacting with others, and firmly believed I was more open-minded than most people I knew (especially the white people I worked with). Given all that, why in the world would I *choose* to sit in a classroom for two days to hear some trainer tell me what I already knew?

That first step onto my diversity path required a willingness to humble myself, to be vulnerable and acknowledge my unconscious incompetence and blind spots – to become a critical thinker. There was so much to learn and I was anxious to become a diversity "expert" as quickly as possible! I read books/magazines/articles, did Internet research and attended D&I conferences. Certainly that was not wasted effort and I continue to engage in those activities. Yet, it is the difficult, uncomfortable, often emotionally charged conversations I have with people (one-on-one and with groups) that truly elevate my level of awareness and understanding around the complexities of diversity and inclusion. Initiating and staying with these conversations does not come naturally for me as I was taught that expressions of anger were taboo and to avoid conflict at all costs, particularly in professional settings. Therein lies what gets in the way of most people having authentic diversity conversations **across difference** (We have diversity conversations with like-minded people all the time). In his book, **Sitting in the Fire,** Arnold Mindell puts it this way; "It costs time and courage to learn how to sit in the fire of diversity. It means staying centered in the heat of trouble." True critical thinkers work hard to "sit in the fire of diversity." Sometimes they come out the other side unscathed, just like they went in; other times they emerge as changed individuals with new beliefs, attitudes and worldviews. Either way, it's a testament to those who are willing to go there!

Wendell C. Ellis

As a second-generation diversity trainer I have, in some form, been traveling along this path since birth.

My earliest memories have a theme that can be described by many adjectives; husky, chubby, chunky and my personal favorite "fluffy". Since age four I have been overweight. I remember shopping in the "husky" section of department stores. The labeled clothes, "one size fits all," failed to say who "all" was. I eclipsed 200 pounds in the fifth grade; 250 pounds in the eighth grade and 340 as a freshman in college. I lived in a world that reminded overweight people every day that it was NOT o.k. to be obese.

As a pre-teen and teenager, I remember how hard it was to compete in a "normal" world. I played organized baseball, basketball and football from age four. I was a three-sport "All-Star"; by sixth grade I had outgrown the uniforms for baseball and basketball, so I focused my attention to football. Being "forced" to make that choice was saddening. All I could think was, "Why can't they make bigger uniforms for people like me?" The world was telling me, "People like you need to lose weight." The challenges of obesity plagued me throughout my high school years.

Miami University was the first time I dated. There was something about playing football that attracted co-eds. I had a sense of humor, a great smile, and personality to boot. Young women at Miami asked me out as I was still self-conscious about my weight.

Managing my personal biases is less challenging when I apply the principles I facilitate and learn as a part of continuing diversity education. For the participants in my diversity classes, that challenge may be more difficult. I've listened to thousands of diversity "horror" stories over the past eleven years. The stories bring a realization that there is still a lot to be done in achieving inclusive work environments. My role is to manage the conversation and facilitate healthy discourse in satisfying the objectives of the course. That can be challenging when participants in your class feel forced into the conversation. Participants often come into class with a hostile posture; many are in denial of the impact of their biases and prejudices in the workplace. You have 8-16 hours for that "aha moment". Your only hope is that something you say, some aspect of your curriculum or the conversation impacts a talented group of staff members.

You have highly educated and talented employees that don't have or want to take time out of their schedule for two days of training. It is my job to create an engaging environment to learn and make the conversation less difficult. However, there are times when the wheels come off and you find yourself in a nightmare.

You never forget your nightmare experiences. One of those moments happened in a training session during a discussion on promotional opportunities. A staff member made a comment about the company's promotional policies, "We seem to promote under-qualified women and minorities just to check the box." Overwhelmingly, the other students shared his perception. He went on to say that recently there had been a promotion of fourteen employees. Of the fourteen staff promoted, thirteen were Hispanic-American. The staff in my class was livid; they viewed the promotion as reverse discrimination. It took all of my diversity skills to manage their anger. I walked them through a conversation by asking several thought provoking questions, that caused them to think about the perspective's held by others.

The conversation that followed challenged them to think critically about their biases in the workplace. For most, this was the "aha moment". The class ended in a great conversation that highlighted the effectiveness of diversity critical thinking and fully engaged staff.

A Towers and Perrin study on engagement concluded that, on average, 20% of the workforce is highly engaged, 60% moderately engaged and 20% disengaged. When you ask managers why 80% of the average workforce works below full engagement, the most popular answers are; job fit, lack of training, unclear direction, poor leadership, and ineffective management. You have to apply critical thinking and problem solving skills. If you have moderate or disengaged staff, it may be beneficial to ask yourself the question, "What might I be missing." It is a theme that all of our senior consultants implore in our training sessions. If you are willing to ask questions and apply the process towards problem solving, you are going a long way in resolving workplace engagement issues and inspiring your staff toward reaching their full potential.

I must own my biases and their impact as I continue along my diversity journey. That awareness enables me to challenge others traveling their diversity journey. Being a part of their journey, I carry a sense of responsibility. When the moment comes where I look across the class and know "they get it," that reminds me why I do the work we do.

Diversity Conversations

Presentation

"Every relationship starts with a conversation"

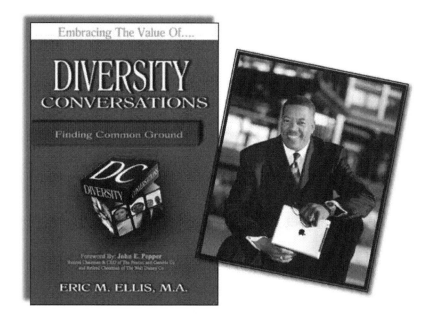

There is no further permission needed prior to delivering this presentation.

Diversity Conversations
Presentation

1   The purpose of this presentation is to provide support for those who are interested in sharing this information with others in their workplace, school and community.

2. We recommend that you read the entire book prior to delivering the presentation.

3. The presentation has captured many of the most important concepts shared in this book. However, feel free to customize the presentation based upon your unique needs.

4. Contact our office if you would like us to email you a copy of this PowerPoint presentation.

We would appreciate you sharing any changes or improvements you make to the presentation. We would also like to hear examples of how you are utilizing the presentation and its effectiveness in serving the needs of various groups of people.

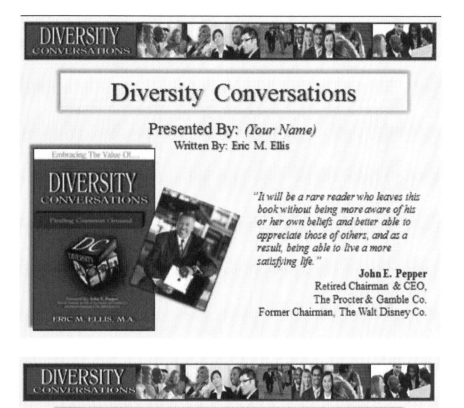

Diversity Conversations

Presented By: *(Your Name)*
Written By: Eric M. Ellis

"It will be a rare reader who leaves this book without being more aware of his or her own beliefs and better able to appreciate those of others, and as a result, being able to live a more satisfying life."

John E. Pepper
Retired Chairman & CEO,
The Procter & Gamble Co.
Former Chairman, The Walt Disney Co.

Diversity Conversations Overview

- Define Diversity
- Define a Diversity Conversation
- Describe Cost & Benefits of Diversity
- Describe the Culture
- Social Challenges & Needs
- Diversity Conversation Goals
- Describe 3 Diversity Conversations
- Becoming a Diversity Critical Thinker
- Applying 'RESPECT'
- Q&A

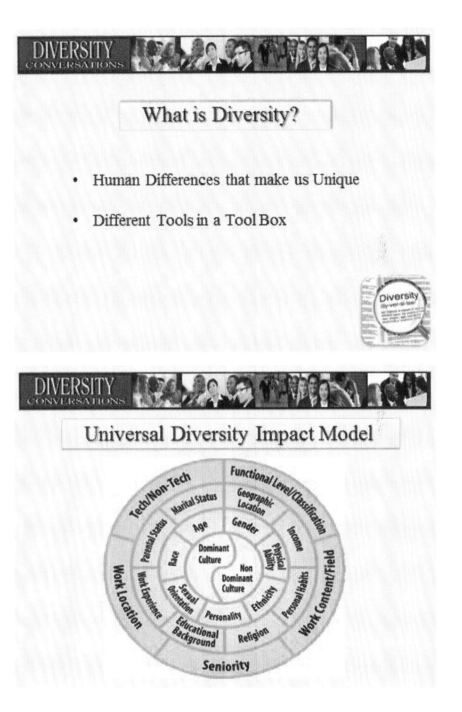

Diversity Exercise

I. How do you define yourself?

II. What are the messages you received about your unique differences and how do those messages impact you today?

Diversity Conversations Defined

Definition:

The conversations that people have internally and with others related to Diversity.

Purpose:

The main objective of the book is to assist people in improving their critical thinking skills in order to engage in more productive discussions about human differences.

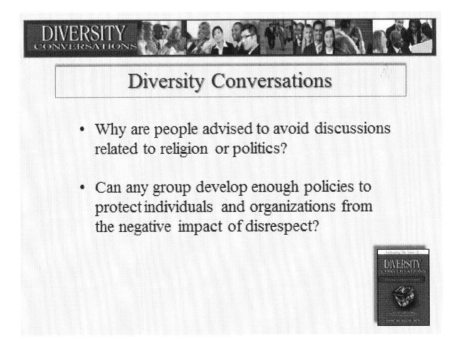

Diversity Conversations

- Almost every relationship begins with a conversation.
- Conversations can go well or poorly.
- Diversity adds emotion to conversations.
- No one succeeds at Diversity Conversations without preparation.
- The goal is to improve our thinking and behavior when responding to diverse people and points of view.

Diversity Conversations

- Why are people advised to avoid discussions related to religion or politics?

- Can any group develop enough policies to protect individuals and organizations from the negative impact of disrespect?

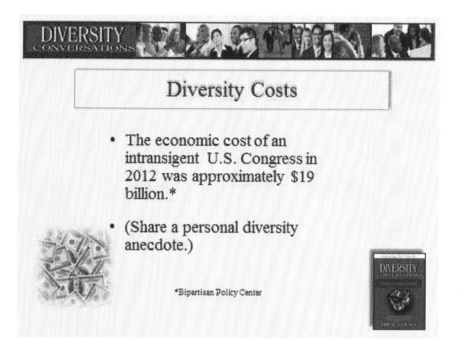

Diversity Costs

- The economic cost of an intransigent U.S. Congress in 2012 was approximately $19 billion.*

- (Share a personal diversity anecdote.)

*Bipartisan Policy Center

The Cost of Disrespect*

Workers on the Receiving End of Disrespect... (800 managers & employees across 17 industries)	
48%	Intentionally decreased their work effort
47%	Intentionally decreased the time they spent at work
38%	Intentionally decreased the quality of their work
80%	Lost work time worrying about the incident
63%	Lost work time avoiding the offender
66%	Said their performance declined
78%	Said their commitment to the organization declined
25%	Said they took their frustrations out on customers

*2011 Georgetown University Study, Dr. Christine Porath & Dr. Christine Pearson

DIVERSITY CONVERSATIONS

Diversity Competence Counts

- A <u>single person</u> who is low in people skills can lower the collective IQ of an entire group.

  (Chris Argyris, 1993)

- <u>90%</u> of our believability and credibility may be based on people skills – not IQ.

  (Mehrobian, A, 1981)

DIVERSITY CONVERSATIONS

Motivation: Building a Business Case

Positive benefits are achieved when organizations are effective at creating inclusive environments.*

• Customer Satisfaction	+39%
• Productivity	+22%
• Profitability	+27%
• Turnover	-22%

*Gallup Workplace Studies

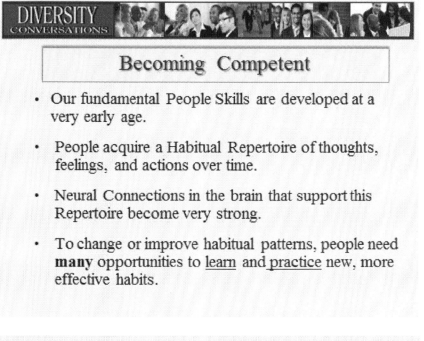

Becoming Competent

- Our fundamental People Skills are developed at a very early age.

- People acquire a Habitual Repertoire of thoughts, feelings, and actions over time.

- Neural Connections in the brain that support this Repertoire become very strong.

- To change or improve habitual patterns, people need **many** opportunities to learn and practice new, more effective habits.

Diversity Competence

Diversity Competence refers to an ability to interact effectively with people of different cultures and socio-economic backgrounds.

Four Components:
1. Awareness of your own Cultural Worldview.
2. Awareness of your attitude towards Cultural Differences.
3. Knowledge of different Cultural Practices & Worldviews.
4. Cross-cultural skills: Developing Cultural Competence results in an ability to understand, communicate with, and effectively interact with people across cultures.

Cultural Observations

- Many people lack significant opportunities to develop respectful relationships across human differences.

- Individuals, organizations, communities and governments are becoming stagnant due to a lack of synergy that often comes from collaboration and compromise.

- Tough economic realities can cause people to focus more on "WIIFM."

Social Challenges

- Sensationalized Media

- Ethnocentric Enculturation

- Sustained Self-Segregation

- Negative Beliefs and Stereotypes

- Fear of Others

Social Needs

- Increased Cultural Awareness
- Identification of major areas where conversations take place about Human Differences
- Identification of existing Mental Models
- Improvement of Diversity Conversations Skills

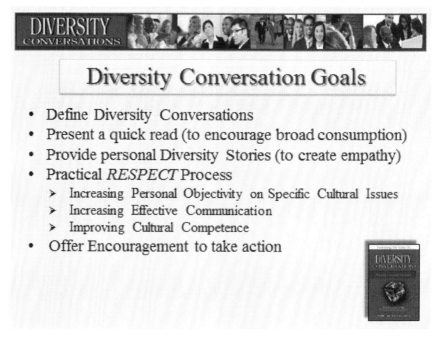

Diversity Conversation Goals

- Define Diversity Conversations
- Present a quick read (to encourage broad consumption)
- Provide personal Diversity Stories (to create empathy)
- Practical *RESPECT* Process
  - ➤ Increasing Personal Objectivity on Specific Cultural Issues
  - ➤ Increasing Effective Communication
  - ➤ Improving Cultural Competence
- Offer Encouragement to take action

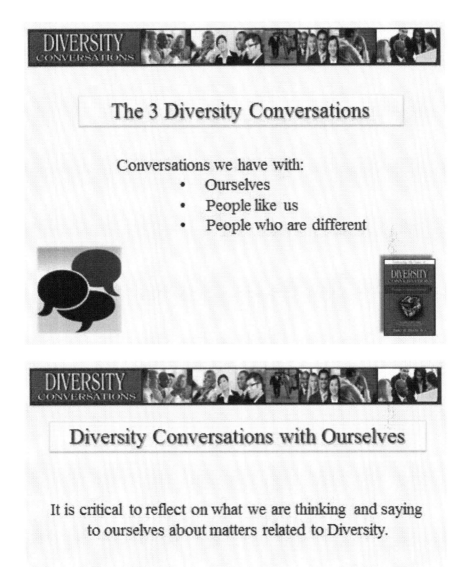

The 3 Diversity Conversations

Conversations we have with:
- Ourselves
- People like us
- People who are different

Diversity Conversations with Ourselves

It is critical to reflect on what we are thinking and saying
to ourselves about matters related to Diversity.

Diversity Conversations with Ourselves

- Engage in Regular Self-Analysis

- Develop a process for gaining Regular Feedback

- Enlist Personal Feedback Coaches

- Develop Intellectual Curiosity

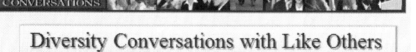

Diversity Conversations with Like Others

- These are conversations that we have with people who are from a diversity perspective like our own.

- It is important to spend time with similar people.

- Interacting with similar people can be affirming.

- However, there are 3 conversations to consider...

Diversity Conversations with Like Others

It is helpful to engage in three types of Diversity Conversations with people like ourselves.

- Conversations of Agreement
- Conversations of Challenge
- Conversations of Questioning

Diversity Conversations with Diverse Others

These are the conversations that we have with people who are different from ourselves.

These conversations have the potential to create significant conflict and counter-productive relationships.

Diversity Conversations with Diverse Others

- De-Stigmatize Prejudice

- Define Four Types of Bias
  - Implicit
  - Explicit
  - Surface-Level
  - Deep-Level

- Strategies for Managing Conflict with Diverse Others

Diversity Critical Thinking

Definition:
An ability to understand and articulate many of the complexities involved in effectively discussing and resolving diversity issues.

Key Behaviors:
- Know your beliefs, principles, and hot buttons
- Search for the truth beyond your common understanding
- Challenge paradigms
- Accept the validity of opposing perspectives
- Accept the uneasiness that accompanies being undecided about an issue or group of people

The RESPECT Process

R   Recognize Diversity Conflicts

E   Evaluate the Strength of Your Beliefs

S   Set a Goal for Diversity Conversations

P   Prepare a DCT Diagram: 2 Major Points of View

E   Establish 3-5 Supporting Points of View

C   Common Ground Statement

T   Take Action to Improve your Diversity Conversations

Putting It All Together

Hot Topics

Topic #1: Valuing vs. Ignoring Differences

Topic #2: Freedom of Speech vs. Culturally-Sensitive Language

Topic #3: Recruiting Diverse Staff vs. it Happening Naturally

Topic #4: Confronting People on Disrespect vs. Ignoring their offenses

Identify Your Unique Topics

Challenges... Frustrations... Needs... Goals...

Special Thanks

It has been said that none of us make it on our own. We are standing on the shoulders of so many who have gone before us. We are also the beneficiaries of the help and support that has been provided by so many whose paths we've crossed. I would like to take this opportunity to mention just a few people and organizations that have provided great support along our journey.

I'd like to give a special thanks to Toyota Motor Manufacturing and Engineering TEMA. Toyota is an amazing company, and we've had the good fortune of serving them as a client since 1996. They have been recognized by Diversity Inc., as one of the top 50 companies for diversity. They have maintained their commitment to diversity through tough economic times. Toyota has a tremendous strategic commitment to diversity and inclusion and we are honored to be a tier one supplier to this great company. Charlotte Neal, the former diversity leader at TEMA, opened the door for our organization and we are so fortunate to have her as a part of our executive team today.

Plante & Moran has been a client of ours for almost a decade. They are regularly listed as one of Fortune Magazines' "Best Places to Work". They are a learning organization and have worked hard to deliver diversity education that makes a difference in their culture.

I am grateful to Wright State University for its support, both as a student athlete and diversity professional. I admire the passion and commitment that the Wright State University community demonstrates to becoming more inclusive. There was no one more supportive of this work than their President, Dr. David R. Hopkins. I am very appreciative to all the client organizations that have utilized our consulting services to strengthen their workplace culture: Wright Paterson Air Force Base: NASIC and AFSAC, Frisch's Restaurant, Kroger Co., Atkore International, Cincinnati Public Schools, Mercy Health Partners, Honda, Lexmark, KMK Law Firm, and Dinsmore & Shohl Law Firm.

I'd also like to mention the following individuals for their support in making this book possible; Allyson Sharp (Editing and Publishing Consultant), Debra Kendrick (Great Editing and new friend), Don and Cheryl Darby (Former Superintendent Princeton Schools), Sarah Cairl (IDC Specialist & Dictation Expert), Jarde Dennis (Illustrator), Tony Tribble (Photographer), Suzanne Collins (IDC Bookkeeper), Charlotte Neal (Diversity Pioneer/Executive), Dr. Sharmella Johnson (Moms), Integrity Development Senior Consultants: Wendell Ellis, Robin Gerald, Barry Myers, Cathy Scrivner, Karen Townsend Ph.D., and Sandy Wheatley. Andy Fishman (Lakota West Teacher & Varsity Girls Basketball Coach), and Nico Tolliver (Lakota West Teacher, Editor). Lynn and Ken Stone (Our friends), Larry Kaiser (Friend & Volunteer), Rev. Freddie.T. Piphus Jr. Zion Global Ministries and Rev. Jonathan Dunn Fresh Anointing Impact (Our Pastors)

Our firm has dedicated a significant amount of time and resources to create, and inspire young people to create music of substance. This musical revolution is aimed at reducing violence and encouraging young artists to use their gifts and talents to uplift themselves, their peers, and the communities in which they live.

For more information, go to www.PositiveMessageMusic.com and download the free mobile phone app available for iPhone or Android phones.

Made in the USA
Charleston, SC
28 July 2013